Ultimate Wit

This book is dedicated to my dear friend,
Grace Duncan, with much love.

Other titles by Des MacHale:

Wit
Wit Hits The Spot
Wit On Target
Wit – The Last Laugh
Wit Rides Again

and look out for:

Wisdom
Irish Wit

Ultimate Wit

Des MacHale

PRION

First published 2002 by
Prion Books Limited
Imperial Works, Perren Street
London NW5 3ED
www.prionbooks.com

ISBN 1-85375-478-1

A catalogue record of this book can be obtained from the
British Library.

Printed and bound in Great Britain
by Creative Print and Design, Wales

Contents

Introduction   7
Art   11
Business and Money   23
Drink and Other Drugs   37
Education   47
Food   59
Lawyers and Other Professions   71
Literature   81
Family and Relations   95
Love, Sex, Marriage, Men and Women   111
Media and Films   133
Medicine and Doctors   153
Music   167
Nationalities and Places   179
Politics   199
Religion   215
Science and Technology   225
Social Behaviour and Manners   241
Sport   263
Theatre and Criticism   279
Miscellaneous   293
Index   305

Introduction

Here it is at last, folks: *Ultimate Wit*, volume six in the *Wit* series, now unquestionably the world's greatest ever collection of sparkling witticisms, wacky wisecracks, humorous quotations, quips, gags, one-liners, droll epigrams, pithy proverbs, hilarious insults, rotten reviews, pernicious put-downs, classic comebacks ... in short, just about the most enjoyable series of books ever published.

All human life is here and we show you the funny side of just about everything – art, business, drink, education, food, lawyers, literature, living, love, media, medicine, music, nationalities, politics, religion, science, social behaviour, sport and theatre, and just in case you think anything is left out, there is a miscellaneous section. We look at the world through the eyes of the great wits of our time – men and women who have perfected their art and who, in the space of a dozen words or so, can reduce you to helpless laughter. You think it's easy? Well, try it some time and see how you compare. Personally, I think being funny is just about the toughest way there is to earn a living, so maybe you and I should just stick to our day jobs for the time being.

Almost nobody takes wit, humour and comedy seriously. Politicians, advertisers and educators sometimes use them as weapons and devices. Writers, actors and comedians earn a living by them. But I believe that wit, humour and comedy (and their hundreds of relatives) are the essence of life. Take them away and what have you got? Seriousness, dullness and boredom. Human beings were made to laugh and a life with lots of laughter is heavenly. Hell may very well be simply life without laughter.

I sincerely hope that *Ultimate Wit* and the other books in this series make you laugh until it hurts, because that's just about the nicest feeling there is – and that includes seeing an old enemy falling from a rooftop.

Des MacHale, Cork, 2002.

Art

Art

If Michelangelo had been heterosexual, the ceiling of the Sistine Chapel would have been painted basic white and with a roller.

Rita Mae Brown

A highbrow is a person who looks at a sausage and thinks of Picasso.

A.P. Herbert

What does this picture represent? It represents two hundred thousand dollars.

Pablo Picasso

Tintoretto will never be anything but a dauber.

Titian

Artists hate the enlightened amateur unless he buys.

Ernest Dimmet

Sodom-hipped young men, with the inevitable sidewhiskers and cigarettes, the faulty livers and the stained teeth, reading Lawrence as an aphrodisiac, and Marie Corelli in their infrequent baths, spew onto paper and canvas their ignorance and perversions, wetting the bed of their brains with discharges of fungoid verse. This is the art of today.

Dylan Thomas

James Whistler once dyed a rice pudding green so that it wouldn't clash with the walls of his dining room.

Geoff Tibballs

Patriotism is the last refuge of the sculptor.

William Plomer

Art dealers are not happy unless they tell twelve lies before lunchtime.

Damien Hirst

Vincent Van Gogh's mother painted all of his best things. The famous mailed decapitated ear was a figment of the public relations firm engaged by Van Gogh's dealer.

Roy Blount

Rembrandt's first name was Beauregard, which is why he never used it.

Dave Barry

I hate all Boets and Bainters.

King George I

A sculpture is just a drawing you fall over in the dark.

Al Hirschfeld

In the mornings, artists work. They fall in love only in the afternoons.

Frederic Raphael

I will be so brief I have already finished.

Salvador Dali

Art

What has Oscar in common with Art? Except that he dines at our tables and picks from our platter the plums for the puddings he peddles in the provinces.

James McNeill Whistler

I suggest they put an acoustical tile ceiling in the Sistine Chapel to cut down on the din produced by German tourists.

Fran Lebowitz

Thank heaven for hypocrites – they keep the arts going.

Mark Twain

Artists, as a rule, do not live in purple; they live mainly in the red.

Lord Pearse

It is well-known that heterosexuality in males in urban areas is caused by overcrowding in artist colonies.

Fran Lebowitz

I've never been to the Louvre, but there are only three works there worth seeing and I've seen colour reproductions of all of them.

Harold Ross

A portrait is a picture in which there is something wrong with the mouth.

Eugene Speicher

You're not meant to understand them – they're bloody works of art.

Sonia Lawson

Rossetti is not a painter. Rossetti is a ladies' maid.

James McNeill Whistler

This painter is a very good painter and observes the Lord's commandments. He hath not made to himself the likeness of anything that is in heaven above or that is in the earth beneath or that is in the waters under the earth.

Abraham Lincoln

If old masters had labelled their fruit, one wouldn't be so likely to mistake pears for turnips.

Mark Twain

The distinction between a genuine and an imitation Turner is a very fine one.

James McNeill Whistler

Pop art is the inedible raised to the unspeakable.

Leonard Baskin

One more word out of you and I'll paint you as you are.

Max Lieberman

A modern sculptor is a man who can take a rough block of stone or wood, work on it for months and make it look like a rough block of stone or wood.

Charles Kelly

Art

Do the security guards in art museums ever really stop anybody from stealing the paintings? Hey, give me back that Cezanne, where do you think you're going with that?

Jerry Seinfeld

Artists do not steal. But they do borrow without giving back.

Ned Rorem

Nothing unites the English like war. Nothing divides them like Picasso.

Hugh Mills

Dada wouldn't buy me a Bauhaus.

John Sloan

The less I behave like Whistler's mother the night before, the more I look like her the morning after.

Tallulah Bankhead

Who is this chap Augustus John? He drinks, he's dirty, and I know there are women in the background.

Bernard Montgomery

At an exhibition of Invisible Art in Tarragona, Spain, a fight broke out between the artist and a man who tried to pay for a £350 blank canvas with an invisible cheque.

Nicholas Parsons

So your mother has a Whistler – now there's a novelty.

Eric Morecambe

Never buy a Van Gogh from a fellow in a mini van while the engine is still running.

Mitch Murray

Sculpture is mudpies which endure.

Cyril Connolly

I have eaten my way to the top. I am a work of art created by the finest chefs in Europe.

Robert Morley

I call my house Lautrec – because it's got two loos.

Tommy Cooper

It might be an idea if Miss Winterson got out her brushes and set to painting her masterpiece as soon as possible. Because the signs are, right now, that she certainly isn't ever going to write one.

Julie Burchill

It is only an auctioneer who can admire all schools of art equally.

Oscar Wilde

One reassuring thing about modern art is that things can't be as bad as they are painted.

Walthall Jackson

Excuse me guard, where is the big Mona Lisa?

Dave Barry

Art

I've been doing a lot of abstract painting lately, extremely abstract. No brush, no paint, no canvas, I just think about it.

Steven Wright

If my husband Picasso ever met a woman in the street who looked like one of his paintings he would faint.

Jacqueline Roque

To the accountants, a true work of art is an investment that hangs on the wall.

Hilary Alexander

Sculpture is what you bump into when you back up to look at a painting.

Ed Reinhart

Art is making something out of nothing and selling it.

Frank Zappa

Varnishing is the only artistic process with which the Royal Academicians are thoroughly familiar.

Oscar Wilde

At the Art Exhibition fruit sold well, and chickens, and items like corks and shoes, though nudes were slow.

Alex Hamilton

Architecture is the art of how to waste space.

Philip Johnson

The workmanship was fairly neat and resembled in many ways the kind of barely ingenious handicraft pursued in hospitals by the disabled, who are anxious to employ their fingers without taxing their intellect or senses.

Evelyn Waugh

They couldn't find the artist so they hung the picture.

Frank Zappa

Last year I went fishing with Salvador Dali. He was using a dotted line. He caught every other fish.

Steven Wright

Art is anything done by a man or woman on paper, canvas or a musical keyboard that people pretend to understand and sometimes buy.

Elbert Hubbard

I sometimes feel as if I have nothing to say and I want to communicate this.

Damien Hirst

A ship ran aground carrying a cargo of red and black paints. The whole crew was marooned.

William Bishop

I just keep painting until I feel like pinching the flesh tones of the nudes. Then I know it's right.

Pierre-Auguste Renoir

Art

He was probably our greatest living painter – until he died.

Will Rogers

Rembrandt is not to be compared in the painting of character with our extraordinarily gifted English artist, Mr Rippingille.

John Hunt

There is a thin line between genius and insanity. I have erased that line.

Oscar Levant

I couldn't have a modern painting hanging in my home. It would be like living with a gas leak.

Edith Evans

There is something wrong with a work of art if it can be understood by a policeman.

Patrick Kavanagh

I believe that a real composer writes for no other purpose than to please himself. Those who compose because they want to please others and have audiences in mind are not artists.

Arnold Schoenberg

The stars are not bad, but there are decidedly too many of them, and they are not very well arranged. I would have done it differently.

James McNeill Whistler

The Arts Council doesn't believe in supporting amateurs, except in its own ranks.

John Drummond

We must remember that art is art. Still, on the other hand, water is water – and east is east and west is west, and if you take cranberries and stew them like apple sauce, they taste much more like prunes than rhubarb does.

Groucho Marx

'Woman with Hat' was a tremendous effort on the part of Matisse, a thing brilliant and powerful, but the nastiest smear of paint I had ever seen.

Leo Stein

Business & Money

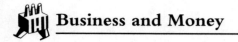

Money is not the most important thing in the world – love is. Fortunately I love money.

Jackie Mason

Don't get mad – get everything.

Ivana Trump

You'd be surprised how much better looking a man gets when you know he's worth a hundred and fifty million dollars.

Joan Rivers

The businessman is a person to whom age brings golf instead of wisdom.

George Bernard Shaw

If you don't believe in the resurrection of the dead, look at any office at closing time.

Robert Townsend

I notice that more and more of our imports seem to be coming from overseas.

George W. Bush

It was said of Andrew Carnegie that he gave money away as silently as a waiter falling down a flight of stairs with a tray of glasses.

Billy Connolly

It's clearly a budget – it's got lots of numbers in it.

George W. Bush

Business and Money

Business clothes are naturally attracted to staining liquids. This attraction is strongest just before an important meeting.

Scott Adams

Mother always said that honesty was the best policy, and money wasn't everything. She was wrong about other things too.

Gerald Barzan

Three years ago I came to Florida without a nickel in my pocket. And now I've got a nickel in my pocket.

Groucho Marx

They say money talks, but all it ever said to me was 'goodbye'.

Cary Grant

The most expensive thing in the world is a girl who is free for the evening.

Sheryl Bernstein

The national debt is a trillion dollars. Who do we owe this money to? Someone named Vinnie?

Robin Williams

Merchandising reached its apogee in the Lux advertisement which portrayed two articles of lingerie which discussed their wearer's effluvia, for all the world like rival stamp collectors.

S. J. Perelman

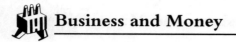

To become a millionaire, what you have to do is to begin as a billionaire. Then go into the airline business.

Richard Branson

No applications can be received here on Sundays, nor any business done during the remainder of the week.

Richard Brinsley Sheridan

I am so changed that my oldest creditors would hardly know me.

Henry Fox

When creating hand-lettered small-business signs you should put quotation marks as in: TRY "OUR" HOT DOG'S.

Dave Barry

I went to the bank and asked to borrow a cup of money. They asked, 'What for?' I said, 'I'm going to buy some sugar.'

Steven Wright

I taught my child the value of a dollar. This week he wants his allowance in yen.

Milton Berle

Will you marry me? How much money do you have? Answer the second question first.

Groucho Marx

The recipe for my success is, some people strike oil, others don't.

J. Paul Getty

I don't want to retire from business. I'd hate to spend the rest of my life trying to outwit an 18-inch fish.

Harold Geneen

To force myself to earn money, I determined to spend more.

James Agate

To steal from one person is theft. To steal from many is taxation.

John Dixon

Xerox has sued somebody for copying.

Dave Letterman

The most difficult of all tasks that a mortal man can embark on is to sell a book.

Stanley Unwin

A typical conversation between me and my teenage daughter runs as follows – 'You need fifty dollars? Forty dollars, what do you need thirty dollars for?'

Bill Cosby

I'm filthy stinking rich – well, two out of three ain't bad.

Emo Philips

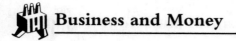

Business and Money

The early bird who catches the worm works for someone who comes in late and owns the worm farm.

John D. MacDonald

I decided long ago never to look at the right-hand side of the menu or the price tag of clothes. Otherwise I would starve, naked.

Helen Hayes

I wasn't always rich. There was a time when I didn't know where my next husband was coming from.

Mae West

All our operators are either drunk or fornicating right now, but if you care to leave a message when you hear the tone...

Hugh Leonard

Who says auditors are human?

Arthur Hailey

If you can afford it, then there is no pleasure in buying it.

Wallis Simpson

A billion dollars is not what it used to be.

J. Paul Getty

I would like to live like a poor person with lots of money.

Pablo Picasso

Business and Money

I was the leading money spender on the PGA Tour.

John Brodie

My husband fell in a river right in front of me and drowned. I rushed to the bank but he had already withdrawn all his money.

Phyllis Diller

Whoever is rich is my brother.

Aristotle Onassis

A manager is a person who looks after visitors so everyone one else can get some work done.

Henry Mintzberg

Money is the root of all evil but man needs roots.

Joe Peers

Bankruptcy is a sacred state, a condition beyond conditions, as theologians might say, and attempts to investigate it are necessarily obscene, like spiritualism.

John Updike

If you can't make your books balance, you take however much they are out by and enter it under the heading ESP, which stands for Error Some Place.

Sam Walton

Money doesn't make you happy. I now have $50 million but I was just as happy when I had $48 million.

Arnold Schwarzenegger

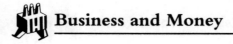

On my income tax form it says 'Check this box if you are blind'. I want to put a check mark about 3 inches away.

> Tom Lehrer

Money can't buy everything. That's what credit cards are for.

> Ruby Wax

Receiving a million dollars tax-free will make you feel better than being flat broke and having a stomach ache.

> Dolph Sharp

Save a little money each month and at the end of the year you'll be surprised at how little you'll have.

> Ernest Haskins

Abolish inheritance tax – no taxation without respiration.

> Bob Schaffer

If you're given a champagne lunch there's a catch somewhere.

> Ben Lyon

Being the boss doesn't make you right, it only makes you the boss.

> Milton Metz

You have to be rich to have a swing like Bing Crosby.

> Bob Hope

Business and Money

My wife has a complex accounting system. She does an initial scan of the supermarket total and says 'Oh my God.' Then she puts the receipt away carefully in a drawer with all the others which ensures that eventually we will have enough receipts to fill a box.

Frank McNally

Have you ever heard of a kid playing accountant, even if he wanted to be one?

Jackie Mason

Do the people who run the stores at airports have any idea what the prices are everywhere else in the world?

Jerry Seinfeld

Lending money to your children is like lending money to a Third World country – you never get the interest back, let alone the principal.

J. L. Long

I found a wallet the other day containing $150. I was going to return it but I thought that if I lost a wallet with $150 in it, what would I want and I realised I would want to be taught a lesson.

Emo Philips

Don't ever stay in bed unless you can make money in bed.

George Burns

My accountant told me to put my money into land so I buried it all in the back garden.

Ken Dodd

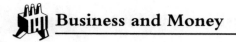

Business and Money

A nickel ain't worth a dime any more.

Yogi Berra

Love is grand. Divorce is a hundred grand.

Mickey Rooney

In my family, the biggest sin was to buy retail.

Woody Allen

Take all the fools out of this world and there wouldn't be any fun living in it, or profit.

Josh Billings

You can name your own salary in this business. I call mine Fred.

Rodney Dangerfield

Isn't it strange? The same people who laugh at gypsy fortune tellers take economists seriously.

J. K. Galbraith

If you can persuade your customers to tattoo your brand name on their chests, they're probably not likely to switch brands.

Harley Davidson

Warning: the dates in the calendar are closer than they appear.

Mary Cecil

It isn't necessary to be rich and famous to be happy. It is necessary only to be rich.

Alan Alda

A mine is a hole in the ground owned by a liar.

Mark Twain

The beatings will continue until morale improves.

Paul Sloane

A vice-president in an advertising agency is a 'molehill' who has until 5pm to make a molehill into a mountain. An accomplished molehill man will often have his mountain finished even before lunch.

Fred Allen

They say money talks. Unfortunately, when it says my name it says 'Who?'

Jackie Mason

Money is round. It rolls away.

Sholem Aleichem

When a man says money can't do anything, that settles it, he hasn't any.

E. W. Howe

A rich man and his daughter are soon parted.

Kin Hubbard

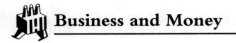

I always pay my alimony on time, because if I ever fall behind, I'm afraid she might try to repossess me.

> Henny Youngman

I got what no millionaire's got, I got no money.

> Gerald F. Lieberman

I have emerged unscathed from the information explosion.

> Henry Martin

A farm is a hunk of land on which, if you get up early enough mornings and work late enough nights, you'll make a fortune – if you strike oil on it.

> Fibber McGee

I could have paid off my debts a lot quicker, but I only did the things I actually believed in myself, like Cranberry Juice Lite.

> Sarah Ferguson

It's very important for folks to understand that when there's more trade there's more commerce.

> George W. Bush

Napoleon was the master of deception. By always holding his hand under his jacket, he fooled everyone into thinking that was where he kept his wallet, when all the time it was in his pants pocket.

> George Burns

Business and Money

They tell me to save for a rainy day. With my luck, I'll save, it'll never rain and I'll be stuck with all that money.

Joe E. Lewis

The referee can't believe he was struck by a pound coin while doing his job. Where did a Celtic fan get that kind of money?

Tam Cowan

I'd like to settle down in my coffin with my credit cards, in case they are needed on the other side. One never knows, and I have always found it unwise to travel without them.

Robert Morley

The buck doesn't stop with me – it doesn't even slow down when it's passing.

Henny Youngman

It is easier to rob by setting up a bank than by holding up a bank.

Bertolt Brecht

Two can live as cheaply as one, and they generally do.

Henny Youngman

I've never been in a situation where having money made it worse.

Clinton Jones

Everybody should pay their income tax with a smile. I tried it but they demanded cash.

Jackie Mason

Drink and Other Drugs

Drink and Other Drugs

The local drink was rakia which gave off a powerful stench, part sewage, part glue.

Evelyn Waugh

Just my luck to have given up drinking when the pubs are staying open all night.

George Best

Can't we just get rid of wine lists? Do we really have to be reminded every time we go out to a restaurant that we have no idea what we are doing? Why don't they just give us a trigonometry quiz with the menu?

Jerry Seinfeld

There is no hangover on earth like the single malt hangover. It roars in the ears, burns in the stomach and sizzles in the brain like a short circuit. Death is the easy way out.

Ian Bell

The human brain can operate only as fast as the slowest brain cells. Excessive intake of alcohol kills brain cells, but naturally it attacks the slowest and weakest brain cells first. In this way, regular consumption of alcohol eliminates the weaker brain cells, making the brain a faster and more efficient machine.

W. C. Fields

Why are so many of my friends recovering alcoholics? Because they can always be relied upon to drive me home.

Jeremy Clarkson

Did you know that if you laid every cigarette smoker end-to-end around the world more than 67 per cent of them would drown?

Steve Altman

I was working as a barman and an American asked me for a traditional Scottish drink. So I gave him 18 pints of lager.

Danny Bhoy

I once shared a house with Errol Flynn. It was called Cirrhosis-by-the-Sea.

David Niven

It was a brilliant affair; water flowed like champagne.

William Evarts

I have practically given up drinking – only about seven bottles of wine and three of spirits a week.

Evelyn Waugh

I never drink unless I'm alone or with someone.

W. C. Fields

It is difficult to speak about proper beer, because its friends are its worst enemies. 'Real ale' fans are just like train spotters – only drunk.

Christopher Howse

Between Scotch and nothing, I suppose I'd take Scotch. It's the nearest thing to good moonshine I can find.

William Faulkner

Beauty is in the eye of the beerholder.

W. C. Fields

Not all chemicals are bad. Without chemicals such as hydrogen and oxygen, for example, there would be no way to make water, a vital ingredient in beer.

Dave Barry

A well-balanced person is someone with a drink in each hand.

Billy Connolly

The first cigar was probably nothing but a bunch of rolled up old tobacco leaves.

Jack Handey

In pubs, spirits are served in mean-spirited measures laughably called singles and doubles. A single is invisible and its presence can be detected only by sniffing the glass. A double whisky can generally be observed through an electron microscope.

Stephen Burgen

Whenever someone asks me if I want water with my Scotch, I say I'm thirsty, not dirty.

Joe E. Lewis

Drink and Other Drugs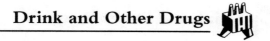

The greatest invention in the history of mankind is beer. Oh, I grant you the wheel was also a fine invention, but the wheel does not go nearly as well with pizza.

Dave Barry

When we drink, we get drunk. When we get drunk we fall asleep. When we are asleep, we commit no sin. When we commit no sin, we go to Heaven. So, let's all get drunk and go to Heaven.

Brian O'Rourke

Never turn down a drink, unless it is of local manufacture.

George Walden

The wine in Scotland was so weak that there were many people who died of dropsies, which they contracted in trying to get drunk.

Samuel Johnson

If I had all the money I've spent on drink, I'd go out and spend it all again on drink.

Vivian Stanshall

You can die from drinking too much of anything – coffee, water, milk, soft drinks and all such stuff as that. And so long as the presence of death lurks with anything one goes through the simple act of swallowing, I will make mine whisky.

W. C. Fields

Drink and Other Drugs

I love drink, so long as it isn't in moderation.

Geoffrey Madan

A guide is a guy who knows where to find whiskey in the jungle.

John Wayne

All my life I have been a very thirsty person.

Keith Floyd

I once saw Michael Scott taking alternate sips of Scotch and Alka Seltzer, thereby acquiring and curing a hangover simultaneously.

Hugh Leonard

My wife clubbed me over the head one night when I came home drunk. It's sweet surprises like that which keep our marriage alive.

Rab C. Nesbitt

Ain't no way I could drink as much as they say I do. Maybe some days I do smoke six packs of cigarettes. Some days maybe I drink twenty to twenty-five beers – but not every day.

Billy Carter

Wine, madame, is God's next best gift to man.

Ambrose Bierce

Drink and Other Drugs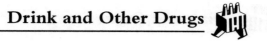

I hate white Burgundies – they so closely resemble a blend of cold chalk soup and alum cordial with an additive or two to bring it to the colour of children's pee.

Kingsley Amis

How well I remember my first encounter with the Devil's Brew. I happened to stumble across a case of bourbon – and went on stumbling for several days thereafter.

W. C. Fields

There was a time when I was into acid and finding the most hip joint in town. Now I'm into antacid and hip joints.

Garrison Keillor

What rascal has been putting pineapple juice in my pineapple juice?

W. C. Fields

Booze is the answer. I don't remember the question.

Denis Leary

Cigarettes are a much cheaper and more widely available alternative to nicotine patches.

Bob Davies

It took a lot of bottle for Tony Adams to admit publicly that he had an alcohol problem.

Ian Wright

Drink and Other Drugs

On some days, my head is filled with such wild and original thoughts that I can barely utter a word. On other days, the liquor store is closed.

Frank Varano

I am as drunk as a lord, but then, I am one, so what does it matter?

Bertrand Russell

Give a man a fish and he will eat for a day. Teach him how to fish, and he will sit in a boat and drink beer all day.

Paul Hawkins

The church is near, but the road is icy. The bar is far, but we will walk carefully.

Yakov Smirnoff

What's so unpleasant about being drunk? You ask a glass of water.

Douglas Adams

One tequila, two tequila, three tequila, floor.

George Carlin

I don't drink water in case it becomes habit-forming.

W. C. Fields

Drinking makes such fools of people, and people are such fools to begin with, that it's compounding a felony.

Robert Benchley

Drink and Other Drugs

In the order named, these are the hardest to control: wine, women and song.

Franklin P. Adams

Although man is already ninety per cent water, the Prohibitionists are not yet satisfied.

Josh Billings

I sold my wife to a guy for a bottle of Scotch and now I wish I had her back because I'm thirsty again.

Henny Youngman

The trouble with jogging is that the ice falls out of your glass.

Martin Mull

The five most beautiful words known to man are 'Have one on the house.'

Wilson Mizner

Cocktails have all the disagreeability of disinfectants without the utility.

Shane Leslie

People are really missing why I did this book. This is about alcoholism, my disease. Two years ago I was dead.

Tony Adams

In the first few weeks of pre-season football training, all you do is just sweat out the alcohol.

Pasi Rautianien

# Drink and Other Drugs

I feel like the fellow who fell into a vat of Guinness: I know exactly what to do, but where to begin?

Brendan O'Mahony

Roses are red,
Carnations are pink,
If I had Sammy Davis's talent,
I wouldn't need to drink.

Dean Martin

Alcohol does not make you fat, it makes you lean, against bars, poles and walls.

W. C. Fields

Education

Education

Butler's Education Act provided for the free distribution of university degrees to the deserving poor.

Evelyn Waugh

I speak about six or seven languages – Spanish, Argentinian, Cuban, Mexican...

Seve Ballesteros

The head cannot take in more than the seat can endure.

Winston Churchill

The historian Henry Adams was the only man in America who could sit on a fence and see himself go by.

E. W. Howe

At Princeton University, we guarantee you satisfaction or you get your son back.

Woodrow Wilson

I managed to fail my 11-plus by refusing point-blank to do a maths paper. I put my hand up, gave it back and said 'I'm sorry, I don't do this'.

Nigella Lawson

The easiest way to change history is to become a historian.

Paul Dickson

Whatever people may say against Cambridge, it is certainly the best preparatory school of Oxford that I know.

Oscar Wilde

Education

I read Shakespeare and the Bible and I can shoot dice. That's what I call a liberal education.

Tallulah Bankhead

I intended to give you students some advice at the beginning of the new academic year, but then I remembered how much is left over from last year unused.

George Harris

Learning is the kind of ignorance distinguishing the studious.

Ambrose Bierce

Oxford is the best of our provincial universities.

Lord Annan

Now let me correct you on a couple of things, OK? Aristotle was not Belgian. The central message of Buddhism is not every man for himself; and the London Underground is not a political movement.

Jamie Lee Curtis

For your information, let me ask you a question.

Marshall McLuhan

University printing presses exist, and are subsidised by the Government for the purpose of producing books which no one can read; and they are true to their high calling.

Francis Cornford

The thing that best defines a child is the total inability to receive information from anything not plugged in.

Bill Cosby

Cultural Studies is the vacuous pondering of the absent.

David Womersley

A seminar is a gathering of purportedly intelligent people who sit around pooling their ignorance until group findings emerge.

Bryan Wilson

Mama, whose views on education were remarkably strict, brought me up to be extremely short-sighted.

Oscar Wilde

The main aim of education should be to send children out into the world with a reasonably sized anthology in their heads so that while seated on the lavatory, waiting in doctors' surgeries, on stationary trains or watching interviews with politicians, they may have something interesting to think about.

John Mortimer

Although this work is History, I believe it to be true.

Mark Twain

Why send your kids to college when for the same money you can take them to Disneyland?

Bruce Lansky

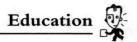

What you don't know would make a great book.

Sydney Smith

If Thomas Edison went to business school, we would all be reading by bigger candles.

Mark McCormack

The world can never be considered educated until we spend as much on books as we do on chewing gum.

Elbert Hubbard

In high school, my sister went out with the captain of the chess team. My parents loved him because they figured that any guy that took hours to make a move was OK with them.

Brian Kiley

Prison holds no terror for me because I lived in Eton in the 1950s.

Jonathan Aitken

Losing money is what university publishing is all about.

Thomas McFarland

Shirley Williams' abolition of grammar schools did more damage to the country than Hitler.

Auberon Waugh

The little I know, I owe to my ignorance.

George Bernard Shaw

Philosophy is like Russia – full of bogs and often invaded by Germans.

Roger Nimier

The task of reviving Irish, we are told, would be hard unless conversations could be limited to requests for food and drink. And who would want conversations on any other subject?

Flann O'Brien

He intended, he said, to devote the rest of his life to learning the remaining twenty-two letters of the alphabet.

George Orwell

My son must have got his brains from his mother, because I've still got mine.

John Brown

A woman in this age is considered learned enough if she can distinguish her husband's bed from that of another.

Hannah Woolley

Did you ever stop to think and forget to start again?

Steven Wright

A college becomes a university when the faculty loses interest in the students.

John Ciardi

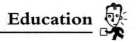

It is a great advantage for a system of philosophy to be substantially true.

George Santayana

Intelligence is what enables you to get along without education; education is what enables you to get along without intelligence.

A.E.Wiggan

Research means they are looking for the guy who lost the file.

Leonard Levinson

Everyone calls 'clear' those ideas which have the same degree of confusion as their own.

Marcel Proust

By the time you're eighty you've learned everything. Too bad you can't remember any of it.

George Burns

You're never too old to stop learning.

Ian Botham

The theoretical broadening which comes from having many humanities subjects on the campus is offset by the general dopiness of the people who study these things.

Richard Feynman

 **Education**

Without education we are in a horrible and deadly danger of taking educated people seriously.

G. K. Chesterton

They say you use only ten per cent of your brain. What about the other ten?

Lara Bliss

The older a man gets, the further he had to walk to school as a boy.

Josh Billings

We all know how stupid the average person is. Now realise that, by definition, 50 per cent of the population is dumber than that.

Ivan Strang

My parents keep asking how school was. It's like saying 'How was that drive-by shooting?' You don't care how it was, you're lucky to be alive.

Angela Chase

We have enough youth – how about a fountain of Smart?

Bob Fuss

A professor is someone who knows more and more about less and less until finally he knows everything about nothing; a student on the other hand learns less and less about more and more until finally he knows nothing about anything.

Leo Moser

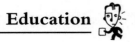

How cruel history can be: here was one of the greatest
thinkers of all time, but all most of us know about him is a
line from a Monty Python song, 'Aristotle, Aristotle, was a
bugger for the bottle.'

Mark Steel

Only intuition can protect you from the most dangerous
individual of all, the articulate incompetent.

Robert Bernstein

His lack of education is more than compensated for by his
keenly developed sense of moral bankruptcy.

Woody Allen

Intellectuals should never marry; they won't enjoy it, and
besides, they should not reproduce themselves.

Don Herold

If you want an example of a moral principle, I would cite
'Do not threaten visiting speakers with a poker.'

Karl Popper

Even if you learn correct English, to whom are you going to
speak it?

Clarence Darrow

Money won't buy happiness, but it will pay the salaries of a
large research staff to study the problem.

Bill Vaughan

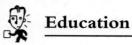

Education

Ideas are like umbrellas. If they are left lying about, they are peculiarly liable to a change of ownership.

Tom Kettle

I am not a man who has read widely, preferring to keep my mind relatively uncluttered with the ideas of others, so that any of my own thoughts may have room to manoeuvre. Unless you have a first-class mind it is a great mistake to afford it a first-class education.

Robert Morley

The effects of youthful education are, like those of syphilis, never completely eradicated.

Robert Briffault

If there's one major cause for the spread of mass illiteracy, it's the fact that everybody can read and write.

Peter DeVries

Men who can speak a number of tongues are notorious for having little to say in any of them.

H. R. Huse

Oxford University is a sanctuary in which exploded systems and obsolete prejudices find shelter after they have been hunted out of every corner of the world.

Adam Smith

You teach a child to read and he or her will be able to pass a literacy test.

George W. Bush

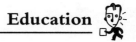

Students achieving Oneness will move on to Twoness.

Woody Allen

I used to be dyslexic but now I'm KO.

Simon Leigh

If that guy counted his balls twice, he'd get two different answers.

Denis Leary

I think the interpreter is the harder to understand of the two.

Richard Brinsley Sheridan

The pluperfect tense had always occasioned him much uneasiness though he has always appeared to the world cheerful and serene.

Sydney Smith

At Wellington School I spent as much time as possible in the sick bay, because it was the sole area of the school in which it was possible to achieve any degree of personal comfort. I shall return to Wellington only if I am allowed to burn the place to the ground.

Robert Morley

Food

Food

Asquith's two lifelong aversions were to eating rabbit and the Roman Catholic Church.

Selina Hastings

I haven't clawed my way to the top of the food chain just to eat vegetables.

Charles Jarvis

I don't even butter my bread; I consider that cooking.

Merla Zellerbach

NAAFI – where you can eat dirt cheap.

Frank Muir

In bush cooking, you always want to garnish when it's off.

Bill Harney

To cook meat, I put a little roast and a big roast in the oven at the same time. When the little one burns, the big roast is done.

Gracie Allen

This restaurant is full at 8.55 p.m. There are obviously a lot of people in Paris who know nothing about food.

Michael Winner

I make a lot of jokes about vegetarians in my act but most of them don't have enough strength to protest.

Ardal O'Hanlon

When I invite a woman to dinner I expect her to look at my face. That's the price she has to pay.

Groucho Marx

If the Chinese are so clever, why can't they do puddings?

Jonathan Ross

I can recommend this restaurant to Hindus out for a good night's fasting.

Denis Leary

Home-made dishes are ones that drive one from home.

Thomas Hood

You'll eat anything when you're a kid – snots, ear wax, toenail clippings, scabs. But not sprouts.

Tony Burgess

This restaurant is very consistent – steak, coffee and ice cream – all the same temperature.

Michael Winner

Never eat any product on which the listed ingredients cover more than one-third of the package.

Herb Caen

I went on a diet – but I had to go on another one at the same time because the first diet wasn't giving me enough food.

Barry Marter

Food

My wife is a light eater; as soon as it's light, she starts eating.

Henny Youngman

The tomato ketchup had a little slip of paper stating 'Inspected by No 12.'

Dave Barry

When I was a child, the family menu consisted of two choices – take it or leave it.

Buddy Hackett

Mother always got offended when I used the word 'puke'. But to me that's what her cooking tasted like.

Jack Handey

My cooking is modern Scottish – if you complain you get headbutted.

Chris Bradley

The English contribution to world cuisine – the chip.

John Cleese

Strength is the capacity to break a chocolate bar into four pieces and then eat just one of them.

Judith Viorst

Cold soup is a very tricky thing and it is the rare hostess who can carry it off. More often than not the dinner guest is left with the impression that had he come only a little earlier he could have gotten it while it was still hot.

Fran Lebowitz

Twenty-four-hour room service generally refers to the length of time it takes for a club sandwich to arrive. This is indeed disheartening, particularly when you've ordered scrambled eggs.

Fran Lebowitz

Poland could live for a year on what my kids leave over from lunch.

Neil Simon

Two cannibals were eating a clown. One said to the other, 'Does this taste funny to you?'

Tommy Cooper

Life is uncertain. Eat dessert first.

Jo Brand

Most vegetarians look so much like the food they eat that they can be classified as cannibals.

Finley Peter Dunne

I never order the soupe du jour in a restaurant. You never know what it is going to be from one day to the next.

Hugh Mulligan

For afternoon tea in England, you are offered a piece of bread that feels like a damp handkerchief and sometimes, when cucumber is added to it, like a wet one.

Compton Mackenzie

Food

Turkey is totally inedible. It's like eating a scrum half.

Willie Rushton

MacHale's Law – in any assortment of mixed biscuits, the chocolate biscuits disappear first.

Des MacHale

Artichoke is a vegetable of which one has more at the finish than at the start of a dinner.

Lord Chesterfield

If I can't have too many truffles I'll do without.

Colette

I'm fed up reading magazine dieting stories about women wearing dresses that could slipcover New Jersey in one photo and thirty days later looking like a well-dressed thermometer.

Erma Bombeck

It was I who introduced bottled water into India.

Barbara Cartland

My wife dresses to kill. She cooks the same way.

Henny Youngman

I did not realise what garlic had done to my breath until one afternoon as I stood waiting for someone to open a door and I noticed that the varnish on the door was bubbling.

Frank Muir

I can't get started in the morning until I've had that first piping hot pot of coffee. Oh I know that there are cooler enemas.

Emo Philips

How can a two-pound box of chocolates make you gain ten pounds?

Roseanne Barr

A great way to lose weight is to eat naked in front of a mirror. Restaurants will almost always throw you out before you can eat too much.

Frank Varano

Sure I eat what I advertise. Sure I eat Wheaties for breakfast. A good bowl of Wheaties with Bourbon can't be beat.

Jay Dean

If it looks like a duck, walks like a duck, talks like a duck, it probably needs a little more time in the microwave.

Lori Dowdy

Inside some of us is a thin person struggling to get out, but she can usually be sedated by a few pieces of chocolate cake.

Jo Brand

It's so beautifully arranged on the plate – you know someone's fingers have been all over it.

Julia Child

Food

Just give me chocolate and nobody gets hurt.

Joan Rivers

Statistics show that fourteen out of every ten women like chocolate.

Sandra Boynton

After sampling my wife's gooseberry flan, I surreptitiously fed it to the dog, who spent the rest of the night in a corner with its paw down its throat.

Les Dawson

There is only one thing worse than a wife who can cook and won't, and that's a wife who can't cook and does.

Mitch Murray

I help my wife with the cooking – I go from room to room removing the batteries from the smoke alarms.

Roy Brown

I remember my Weight Watchers weekly meetings – three hundred of the fattest people in the area would gather every week in one room to discuss their common problem – how to get out of the room.

Totie Fields

Last Christmas I spent over two hours trying to stuff the turkey – I nearly killed it.

Gracie Allen

I have only one rule about food – if it's not chocolate, it's a vegetable.

Carole Cook

Put cream and sugar on a fly and it tastes very much like a raspberry.

E. W. Howe

It must be nice to run a boarding house and not have to worry about something different for dinner every day.

Kin Hubbard

Animals are my friends – I do not eat my friends.

George Bernard Shaw

I will not eat Chinese food with knitting needles because I do not knit with a fork.

Miss Piggy

The first time my husband asked me for an aspirin and a glass of water I knew exactly what to do – I phoned my mother for the recipe.

Gracie Allen

I have steered clear of salad bars, the standard source of a take-out Manhattan lunch, since I spotted an elderly man's nose release a solitary drip on to some cottage cheese.

Joanna Coles

I am not a glutton – I am a food explorer.

Erma Bombeck

Food

I've joined a Keep Fat Club. Every Wednesday morning we meet and eat as many cakes as we can manage.

Jo Brand

The garden is one of a vast number of free outdoor restaurants operated by charity-minded amateurs in an effort to provide healthful, balanced meals for birds, animals and insects.

Henry Beard

In future in restaurants I propose to arm myself with a peacock's feather and place it on the table beside me when I call for the bill. If my credit is questioned I shall employ it in the best Roman manner and simply sick up.

Robert Morley

A chop is a piece of leather skilfully attached to a bone and administered to the patients at restaurants.

Ambrose Bierce

I am a lifelong enemy of tapioca.

Robert Morley

Any dish that has either a taste or an appearance that can be improved by parsley is ipso facto a dish unfit for human consumption.

Ogden Nash

Health food makes me sick.

Calvin Trillin

Turkey has practically no taste except a dry fibrous flavour reminiscent of a mixture of warmed-up plaster of Paris and horse hair. The texture is like wet sawdust and the whole vast feathered swindle has the piquancy of a boiled mattress.

William Connor

I didn't have enough money to buy food. There were times when I had to live on what the audience threw at me.

George Burns

Rhubarb is the vegetable essence of stomach ache.

Ambrose Bierce

Foods used for medicinal purposes such as hot chocolate, brandy, toast and Sara Lee cheesecake have no calories.

Lewis Grizzard

For me two of the most awful words in the English language have always been 'just coffee'.

Robert Morley

Airlines are so considerate – they give you such small portions of their food.

P. J. O'Rourke

I went out to dinner the other night and surprised everyone by ordering the entire meal in French: it was a Chinese restaurant.

Tommy Cooper

Lawyers and Other Professions

Lawyers and Other Professions

Economics is the only profession where you can gain great eminence without ever being right.

George Meany

Lawyers are like rhinoceroses: thick-skinned, short-sighted and always ready to charge.

David Mellor

He might have brought an action against his countenance for libel, and won heavy damages.

Charles Dickens

I didn't steal it. It was 'differently acquired'.

Sara Cytron

I have forgotten more law than you ever knew, but allow me to say, I have not forgotten much.

John Maynard

My father, a teacher at an inner-city comprehensive, once taught a family where all five boys were named Eugene so as to confuse the police.

Joanna Coles

My lawyer is so good they've named a loophole after him.

Steven Wright

A solicitor is a man who calls in a person he does not know, to sign a contract he hasn't seen to buy a property he does not want with money he hasn't got.

Dingwall Bateson

Lawyers and Other Professions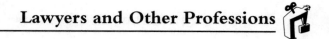

A historian is merely an unsuccessful novelist but then so are most novelists.

H. L. Mencken

Capital punishment would be more effective as a preventive measure if it were administered prior to the crime.

Woody Allen

Remember at the Preston A. Mantis Consumers Retail Law Outlet, our motto is: 'It is very difficult to disprove certain kinds of pain.'

Dave Barry

A cavity is a tiny hole in your child's tooth that takes many, many dollars to fill.

Bill Dodds

You have the right to remain silent, so please shut up.

Denis Leary

He had faced death in many forms but he had never faced a dentist. The thought of dentists gave him just the same sick horror as the thought of Socialism.

Evelyn Waugh

Good news – they've found Hitler. He's alive, living in Buenos Aires and they're bringing him to trial. The bad news – they're holding the trial in L.A.

Alice Kahn

Lawyers and Other Professions

My dental hygienist is cute. Every time I visit, I eat a whole packet of cookies while waiting in the lobby. Sometimes she has to cancel the rest of the afternoon's appointments.

Steven Wright

Homicide of pedestrians was legalised for the benefit of motorists.

L. P. Hartley

As you can see by my suit and the fact that I have all these books of equal height on the shelves behind me, I am a trained legal attorney.

Dave Barry

I don't want to know what the law is, I want to know who the judge is.

Roy Cohn

My wife and I have just celebrated our thirtieth wedding anniversary. If I had killed her the first time I thought about it I'd be out of jail by now.

Les Dawson

I have the kind of lawyer you hope the other fellow has.

Raymond Chandler

I will not prosecute the Earl of Rochester. The more you stir a turd, the more it stinks.

King Charles II

Lawyers and Other Professions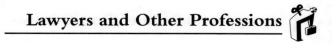

I didn't do it, nobody saw me do it, you can't prove anything.

Bart Simpson

Where there's a will there's a lawsuit.

Addison Mizner

Prison will not work until we start sending a better class of people there.

Laurence J. Peter

If the police arrest a mime, do they tell him he has the right to remain silent?

Steven Wright

An architect's most useful tools are an eraser at the drawing board and a wrecking bar at the site.

Frank Lloyd Wright

We should keep the Panama Canal. After all we stole it fair and square.

S. I. Hayakawa

She broke a leg while visiting London, probably sliding down a barrister.

Dorothy Parker

Selective inbreeding and cloning seem to be producing a traffic warden breed of indeterminate sex but usually with bad complexions.

Leonard Rossiter

Lawyers and Other Professions

If it weren't for golf, I'd probably be a caddie today.

George Archer

The most fun thing a lawyer can do is to say 'I object'.

Jerry Seinfeld

A legislator is an official who spends half his energies making laws and the other half helping his friends to evade them.

Leonard Levinson

I call my attorney Necessity because he knows no law.

Benjamin Franklin

A lawyer swimming safely through shark-infested waters – that's professional courtesy.

John Mortimer

Why does the pharmacist have to be two and a half feet above everyone else? Who the hell is he? He's just a stockboy with pills. Spread out, give me some room. I'm taking pills from this big bottle and I'm putting them in this little bottle.

Jerry Seinfeld

Banking is a career from which no man really recovers.

J. K. Galbraith

When people ask me where I was when Kennedy was shot, I have to admit that I don't have an alibi.

Emo Philips

Lawyers and Other Professions

And God said: 'Let there be Satan, so people don't blame everything on me. And let there be lawyers so people don't blame everything on Satan.'

George Burns

We will hang you, never fear, most politely, most politely.

W. S. Gilbert

Lawyers believe a man is innocent until proven broke.

Robin Hall

The terrible thing about being a football agent is that players get eighty per cent of my earnings.

Eric Hall

During job interviews, when they ask: 'What is your worst quality?' I always say : 'Flatulence.' That way I get my own office.

Dan Thompson

The Law Society prohibits sex between lawyers and their clients to prevent clients for being billed twice for essentially the same service.

Alan Davies

My cousin just died – he was only nineteen. He was stung by a bee – the natural enemy of the tightrope walker.

Dan Rather

After the grand jury session, Vernon Jordan told reporters that he answered the questions truthfully and to the best of his ability. Well, come on, which is it?

David Letterman

It was so cold last winter that I saw a lawyer with his hands in his own pockets.

Henny Youngman

I had a boring office job. I used to clean all the windows in the envelopes.

Rita Rudner

If crime fighters fight crime and fire fighters fight fire, what do freedom fighters fight? They never mention that part to us do they?

George Carlin

I have a fool-proof plan for never having to work – in the event of an interview, wear flip-flops.

Alan Davies

I'm not really concerned with stalking because most of my stalkers would have walkers and canes.

Phyllis Diller

Make Norbury a bishop, or even an archbishop, but not a Chief Justice.

Lord Clare

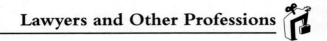

Ignorance of the law excuses no man – from practising it.

Addison Mizner

There is nothing like a solemn oath. People always think you mean it.

Norman Douglas

Women should not sit on juries; no woman will believe that a witness wearing the wrong hat can be giving the right evidence.

James Agate

I'm not saying all publishers have to be literary but some interest in books would help.

N. Wilson

The difference between a lawyer and a computer is that computers get twice as intelligent and half as expensive every two years.

Dorothy Josipovich

Literature

 **Literature**

One should never read the latest books. Instead, wait for a few years and watch most of them disappear into well-deserved oblivion. This eliminates much unnecessary reading.

Somerset Maugham

Seamus Heaney couldn't write out a shopping list without winning some kind of award.

Cosmo Landesman

I am writing a history of the QE2. I have a good track record with larger-than-life Iron Ladies.

Carol Thatcher

The material of *A Tourist in Africa* was so thin that I suggested to Chapman and Hall that I insert adverbs before all the adjectives in an attempt to lengthen the text.

Evelyn Waugh

Max Beerbohm has the most remarkable and deductive genius – and I should say about the smallest in the world.

Lytton Strachey

I found nothing wrong with Gertrude Stein's autobiography except her poor choice of subject.

Clifton Fadiman

David Halberstam's book on the 1950s, called *The Fifties*, is as inspired and clever as its title.

John Podhoretz

I'm a lousy writer but a helluva lot of people have lousy taste.

Grace Metalous

Fine writing, next to doing nothing, is the best thing in the world.

John Keats

The literary biography is the Meals-on-Wheels service of the book world.

Sheridan Morley

I called my first book 'Collected Works Vol 1'.

Max Beerbohm

Henry Miller is not really a writer but a non-stop talker to whom someone has given a typewriter.

Gerald Brenan

They say my writings have made me immortal. But what is the use of immortality to a man when he's dead?

George Moore

The most violent action W. H. Auden ever saw was when he was playing table tennis at Tossa del Mar on behalf of the Spanish Republicans – apart from the violent exercise he got with his knife and fork.

Roy Campbell

He did nothing; he was a poet.

Sheila Mooney

 **Literature**

Anyone could write a novel given six weeks, pen, paper, and no telephone or wife.

Evelyn Waugh

Did you know that Jane Austen had an unpublished manuscript in her drawers called Farts and Flatulence?

Patrick Murray

I have crossed out the parts of your script that I did not like. What I haven't crossed out I'm not happy with.

Cecil B. De Mille

Literature is written material that, a hundred years after the death of the author, is forced upon high school students.

Tom Clancy

That's Kingsley Amis, and there's no known cure.

Robert Graves

Circumlocution is a literary trick whereby the writer who has nothing to say breaks it gently to the reader.

Ambrose Bierce

If it were thought that anything I wrote were influenced by Robert Frost, I would take that particular piece of mine, shred it, and flush it down the toilet, hoping not to clog the pipes.

James Dickey

I became a writer in the same way that a woman becomes a prostitute. First I did it to please myself, then I did it to please my friends and finally I did it for money.

Ferenc Molnar

Substitute 'damn' every time you're inclined to write 'very'; your editor will delete it and the writing will be just as it should be.

Mark Twain

There is only one way to make money at writing and that is to marry a publisher's daughter.

George Orwell

The world's thinnest book is *My Plan To Find The Real Killers* by O. J. Simpson.

Mike McQueen

Edward Gibbon is an ugly, affected, disgusting fellow, and poisons our literary club for me. I class him among infidel wasps and venomous insects.

James Boswell

I would rather endure the pain of a kidney stone the size of a golf ball than to be forced to read this book again.

Ronald Berk

The best place for a female author to discuss terms with an editor is in bed after a couple of double martinis.

Donald MacCampbell

Times are bad. Children no longer obey their parents and everyone is writing a book.

Cicero

To save my mother from the electric chair I couldn't read three pages of James Cavell's The Silver Stallion.

Dorothy Parker

The foundation of T. S. Eliot's work was self-contempt, well-grounded.

F. R. Leavis

You can't fake bad writing. It's a gift.

Richard Le Gallienne

Writing about travels is nearly always tedious, travelling being, like war and fornication, exciting but not interesting.

Malcolm Muggeridge

Censors read a book only with great difficulty, moving their lips as they puzzle out each syllable, when someone tells them that the book is unfit to be read.

Robertson Davies

Sinclair Lewis was a writer who drank, not, as so many have believed, a drunk who wrote.

James Lundquist

Audiences don't know anybody writes a picture. They think the actors just make it up as they go along.

William Holden

Comedy writing is a very difficult competitive job and I say to aspiring writers, 'Don't do it. Don't do it.'

Mel Brooks

I see Sylvia Plath as a kind of Hammer films poet.

Philip Larkin

Truman Capote's book, *In Cold Blood*, when it came out in 1965, was considered an instant classic, largely because Capote told everyone it was.

Bill Bryson

Literature is an occupation in which you have to keep proving your talent to people who have none.

Jules Renard

Authors have the power to bore people long after we are dead.

Sinclair Lewis

It's red hot, mate. I hate to think of this sort of book getting into the wrong hands. As soon as I've finished it, I shall recommend they ban it.

Tony Hancock

Autobiography is the most respectable form of lying.

Humphrey Carpenter

The book of mine enemy has been remaindered. And I am pleased.

Brian James

# Literature

If you are of the opinion that the contemplation of suicide is sufficient evidence of a poetic nature, do not forget that actions speak louder than words.

Fran Lebowitz

I have two very cogent reasons for not printing any list of subscribers – one, that I have lost all the names, – the other, that I have spent all the money.

Samuel Johnson

This year marks the fiftieth anniversary of Barbara Cartland's loss of virginity.

Auberon Waugh

I hate writing. On the other hand, I'm a great believer in money.

S. J. Perelman

Punch is the official journal of dentists' waiting rooms.

Alan Coren

Homer sometimes nods and Wordsworth sometimes wakes.

George Gordon

When I wrote that poem only God and I knew what it meant; now God alone knows.

Friedrich Klopstock

Mein Kampf is the only honest book ever written by a politician.

W. H. Auden

I am immersed in Winston Churchill's brilliant autobiography, disguised as a history of the universe.

A.J. Balfour

Mr Hope should avoid humour, at which he certainly does not excel. His attempts of that nature are among the most serious parts of the book.

Sydney Smith

My husband will never chase another woman. He's too fine, too decent, too old.

Gracie Allen

There must be something about Jeffrey Archer that attracts women but I can't for the life of me see what it is.

Joanna Trollope

Alfred Lawn Tennyson.

Valerie Grove

I find that a bookstore is a wonderful laxative.

Jerry Seinfeld

Will I write my autobiography? On what?

Chris Eubank

Oscar Wilde had nothing to say and he said it.

Ambrose Bierce

Literature

I'm not going to get into the ring with Tolstoy.

Ernest Hemingway

Barbara Cartland is an animated meringue.

Arthur Marshall

Life is one fool thing after another, whereas love is two fool things after each other.

Oscar Wilde

The freelance writer is a person who is paid per piece or per word or perhaps.

Robert Benchley

It is a pity that critics should show so little sympathy with writers, and curious when we consider that most of them tried to be writers themselves, once.

Max Beerbohm

The book collector's motto – Never lend a book; never give a book away; never read a book.

John Sparrow

Churton Collins is a louse in the locks of literature.

Alfred Tennyson

It would be no loss to the world if most of the writers now writing had been strangled at birth.

Rebecca West

Literature

Everyone but Somerset Maugham said I was a second Somerset Maugham, with the exception of a few who preferred to describe me as a second Sacha Guitry.

Noël Coward

Margot Asquith's autobiography came in four volumes, neatly boxed, suitable for throwing purposes.

Dorothy Parker

Wasn't it Shakespeare who said 'Brevity is the soul of wit' and then went on to write plays that last four and a half hours?

Mitch Murray

The best part of the fiction in many novels is the notice that the characters are all purely imaginary.

Franklin P. Adams

He grew so proficient in poetry that he could write a sonnet of almost any length at a moment's notice.

Wallace Irwin

We didn't have metaphors in our day. We didn't beat about the bush.

Fred Trueman

There ain't nothing that breaks up homes, country and nations like somebody publishing their memoirs.

Will Rogers

A footnote is like running downstairs to answer the doorbell during the first night of marriage.

John Barrymore

Solzhenitsyn is a bad novelist and a fool. The combination usually makes for great popularity in the US.

Gore Vidal

If length be not considered a merit, *Paradise Lost* has no other.

Edmund Waller

If you take hyphens seriously you will surely go mad.

John Benbow

My attitude to public relations is don't tell the bastards anything.

William Faulkner

Waterstone's Literary Diary records the birthdays of notable contemporary figures. My own birthday, May 9th, is blank except for the note: first British Launderette is opened on Queensway, London 1949.

Alan Bennett

Publishers and authors seem to think that the smaller the child, the larger the book should be.

Penelope Mortimer

Fiction requires truth-telling, whereas in a biography one can make things up.

Peter Ackroyd

Some day I intend to read all those books I have written.

Dan Quayle

An agent is someone whom you pay to make bad blood between you and your publisher.

Angela Thirbell

J. W. Cross's *Life of George Eliot* is not a Life at all. It is a Reticence, in three volumes.

W. E. Gladstone

Poetry is sissy stuff that rhymes. Weedy people say la and fie and swoon when they see a bunch of daffodils.

Geoffrey Willans

Frankenstein is a book about what happens when a man tries to have a baby without a woman.

Anne Mellor

The endings to most volumes of non-fiction currently produced in this country are being fixed by overseas betting syndicates.

Armando Iannucci

Family and Relations

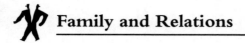

With my luck, if I went into the pumpkin business, they'd probably outlaw Hallowe'en.

Larry Ziegler

Dudley Moore is my son – my smallest son.

Roger Moore

George Burns is old enough to be his father.

Red Buttons

My parents were so strict we weren't allowed to read *Goldilocks and the Three Bears*. It wasn't so much Goldilocks going into all those beds as the implied marital tension in the bear family.

Ardal O'Hanlon

To me, funerals are like bad movies. They last too long, everybody is overacting and the ending is completely predictable.

George Burns

Ashes to ashes and clay to clay; if the enemy don't get you, your own folk may.

James Thurber

Even if you haven't got a baby, when you're going out, hire a babysitter. As you're leaving say, 'check out the baby in about half an hour'. Better still, mark one of the rooms 'Baby's room', and leave the window open with a little rope ladder hanging out.

Harry Hill

Family and Relations

If you let that sort of thing go on, your bread and butter will be cut from right under your feet.

Ernest Bevin

I'd like to marry a nice, domesticated homosexual with a fetish for wiping down formica and different vacuum-cleaner attachments.

Jenny Eclair

Families is where our nation finds hope, where wings take dream.

George W. Bush

My mother from time to time puts on her wedding dress. Not because she's sentimental. She just gets really far behind in her laundry.

Brian Kiley

If the child is a boy, he is to be named James; if a girl, it would be kinder to drown her.

Evelyn Waugh

No man was ever so low as to have respect for his brother-in-law.

Finley Peter Dunne

Where have you been, who've you been with, what have you been doing and why?

Arthur Lucan

⚔ Family and Relations

My favourite way to wake up is to have a certain French movie star whisper to me softly at two-thirty in the afternoon that if I want to get to Sweden in time to pick up my Nobel Prize for literature, I had better ring for breakfast.

Fran Lebowitz

My new son has a face like that of an ageing railway porter who is beginning to realise that his untidiness has meant that he'll never get that ticket-collector's job he's been after for twenty years.

Kingsley Amis

It was our son that kept our marriage together – neither of us wanted custody of him.

Chubby Brown

I was an unwanted child. When my parents gave me a rattle it was still attached to the snake.

Joan Rivers

You know your children are growing up when they stop asking you where they come from and refuse to tell you where they are going.

P. J. O'Rourke

There are only three occasions in Ireland when you'll find the whole family together – a wedding, a funeral, or if I've brought home a bag of chips.

Ardal O'Hanlon

An advantage of having only one child is that you always know who did it.

Erma Bombeck

You feel completely comfortable entrusting your baby to your parents for long periods, which is why most grandparents flee to Florida at the earliest opportunity.

Dave Barry

Whatever is on the floor will wind up in the baby's mouth. Whatever is in the baby's mouth will wind up on the floor.

Bruce Lansky

If Abraham's son had been a teenager, it wouldn't have been a sacrifice.

Scott Spendlove

Do not, on a rainy day, ask your child what he feels like doing because I assure you that what he feels like doing, you won't feel like watching.

Fran Lebowitz

You know your family is really stressed when conversations often begin with 'Put the gun down and then we can talk.'

Mike McQueen

Say what you like about Genghis Khan but when he was around, old ladies could walk the streets of Mongolia safely at night.

Jo Brand

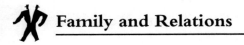

Where did you go? Out. What did you do? Nothing.

Richard Armour

If you cannot open a childproof bottle, use pliers or ask a child.

Bruce Lansky

Freud is all nonsense; the secret of all neurosis is to be found in the family battle of wills to see who can refuse longest to help with the dishes.

Julian Mitchell

A friend of mine was caring for his mother as her Alzheimer's disease progressed. When the time came to discuss her burial wishes, he asked whether she wanted to be cremated or buried. His mother replied, 'Surprise me.'

Allen Klein

My friend Winnie is a procrastinator. He didn't get his birthmark until he was eight years old.

Steven Wright

When your first baby drops its pacifier, you sterilize it. When your second baby drops its pacifier, you tell the dog 'Fetch'.

Bruce Lansky

In spite of the seven thousand books of expert advice, the right way to discipline a child is still a mystery to most fathers and mothers. Only grandmother and Genghis Khan know how to do it.

Bill Cosby

Family and Relations

If you wonder where your child left his roller skates, try walking around the house in the dark.

Leopold Fechtner

You know children are growing up when they start asking questions that have answers.

John Plomp

We've been having some trouble with the school bus. It keeps bringing the kids back.

Bruce Lansky

When I have a kid, I'm going to get one of those strollers for twins. Then put the kid in and run around, looking frantic. When he gets older, I'll tell him he used to have a brother, but he didn't obey.

Steven Wright

It's amazing. One day you look at your phone bill and realise your children are teenagers.

Milton Berle

My socks DO match. They're the same thickness.

Steven Wright

I was doing the family grocery shopping accompanied by two children, an event I hope to see included in the Olympics in the near future.

Anna Quindlen

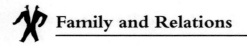# Family and Relations

My mother phones daily to ask, 'Did you try to reach me?' When I reply, 'No,' she adds, 'So, if you're not too busy, call me while I'm still alive,' and hangs up.

Erma Bombeck

I lost my parents on the beach when I was a kid. I asked a lifeguard to help me find them. He said, 'I don't know, kid, there are so many places they could hide.'

Rodney Dangerfield

You're a disgrace to our family name of Wagstaff, if such a thing is possible.

Groucho Marx

A wonderful woman my grandmother – eighty-six years old and not a single grey hair on her head. She's completely bald.

Dick Bentley

A man has six items in his bathroom: a toothbrush, shaving cream, razor, a bar of soap and a towel from the Holiday Inn. The average number of items in the typical woman's bathroom is 337. A man would not be able to identify most of these items.

Dave Barry

I love all my children, but some of them I don't like.

Lillian Carter

Not a single member of the under-age set has yet to propose the word chairchild.

Fran Lebowitz

The greatest single cause of unhappiness in Britain today is the modern British woman's hatred of housework.

Auberon Waugh

If you see a well-dressed man you know at once his wife is good at picking out clothes.

Joan Rivers

Children aren't happy with nothing to ignore, and that's what parents were created for.

Ogden Nash

A woman who does a man's work is just a lazy cow.

Jo Brand

A self-made man is one who believes in luck and sends his son to Oxford.

Christina Stead

For most of history, baby-having was in the hands of women. Many fine people were born under this system.

Dave Barry

Adolescence is a time of rapid change. Between the ages of twelve and seventeen, for example, a parent can age as much as twenty years.

Dale Baughman

Life is like a dog-sled team. If you ain't the lead dog, the scenery never changes.

Lewis Grizzard

Family and Relations

Mixed-faith marriages were frowned upon in Killcock. Both parents had to sign a declaration that any babies that resulted from the union had to be brought up as children.

James McKeon

Never give your boy all the allowance you can afford. Keep some in reserve to bail him out.

Josh Billings

Everyone knows how to raise children except the people who have them.

P. J. O'Rourke

Children have become so expensive that only the poor can afford them.

Mark Twain

You can always get someone to love you – even if you have to do it yourself.

Tom Masson

If I had to choose between my wife and my putter – I'd miss her.

Gary Player

In the algebra of psychology, X stands for a woman's mind.

Ambrose Bierce

I long for my baby boy to be a homosexual because homosexuals are so good to their mothers.

Ruth Sansom

Chloe has just expressed herself all over the floor.

Hannah Betts

I have a horror of leaving this world and not having anyone in the family know how to replace a toilet-roll holder.

Erma Bombeck

What women want is men, careers, money, children, friends, independence, freedom, respect, love, and a three-dollar pantyhose that won't run.

Phyllis Diller

My mother joined the peace corps when she was seventy; my sister Gloria is a motorcycle racer; my other sister Ruth is a holy roller preacher and my brother Jimmy thinks he's going to be President of the United States. Shucks, I'm really the only normal one in the family.

Billy Carter

I told my child there were two words I wanted her never to use – one was 'swell' and the other was 'lousy'. 'OK mum,' she said, 'What are the words?'

Phyllis Diller

Bluebeard was a husband with the neatest solution to the alimony problem.

Leonard Levison

Whoever said you can't take it with you has never seen the family car packed for a vacation trip.

Lester Klimek

Family and Relations

When I was a kid the order of the bath was first the kids, then the whippets, then grandad.

Ken Dodd

A pedestrian is a man who has two cars – one being driven by his wife and the other by one of his teenage children.

Robert Bradbury

I was a bottle baby – then one day I pushed the cork out and escaped.

Ken Dodd

My grandfather was cut down in the prime of his life. My grandmother used to say that if he had been cut down fifteen minutes earlier, they could have resuscitated him.

Mark Twain

I was sleeping alone the other night, thanks to the exterminator.

Emo Philips

At the funeral of a ninety-year-old Irish woman, by the graveside her son-in-law collapsed and had to be rushed to hospital. This naturally cast a gloom over the entire proceedings.

John Murphy

A family is a group of people with the same genes – which means that only one of them can go out at a time.

Ken Dodd

My mother never saw the irony of calling me a son-of-a-bitch.

Jack Nicholson

I married your mother because I wanted children. Imagine my disappointment when you came along.

Groucho Marx

The best way to keep children at home is to make the home atmosphere pleasant and to let the air out of their tyres.

Dorothy Parker

Babies don't need the traditional slap on the rear end when they are born. But at least it gives them a good idea of what life is going to be like.

P. J. O'Rourke

It cannot be mere coincidence that the anagram of MOTHER IN LAW is WOMAN HITLER.

Les Dawson

My dad was the fastest man in the world. He didn't quit work until five o'clock and he was always home by two.

Ken Dodd

People on dates shouldn't be allowed out in public.

Jerry Seinfeld

My father was a man of great principle, though what those principles were I cannot say.

Eugene O'Neill

Family and Relations

Heredity is the thing a child gets from the other side of the family.

Marcelene Cox

A good father lives so he is a credit to his children.

Arnold Glasow

When my mother-in-law hangs out her bra to dry, we lose an hour of daylight.

Les Dawson

What a wonderful day it is for grandad-baiting – stick a rabbit and a ferret down his trousers and see how long it is before his eyes cross.

Ken Dodd

After I saw the movie *Roots*, I tried to trace my family but they wouldn't lie down on the paper.

Richard Pryor

To the best of my knowledge there has been no child in space. I would like to learn about being weightless and I'd like to get away from my mother's cooking.

Jonathan Adashek

Here is a message for all you parents. Is your teenage son or daughter out for the evening? If so, take advantage of the opportunity. Pack your furniture, call a moving van, and don't leave a forwarding address.

Henny Youngman

Family and Relations

A 'good' family, it seems, is one that used to be better.

Cleveland Amory

My wife complained that the kids hardly see me any more. I said 'Kids?'

Mitch Murray

Having children is painful. I screamed so loudly I woke up the whole neighbourhood – and that was just during conception.

Joan Rivers

I'm still young enough to want to find a woman to have my children because frankly I'm pissed off with them.

Mitch Murray

One of my friends asked me if a woman should have children after 35. I said that I thought 35 children is enough for any woman.

Gracie Allen

My wife and I were never blessed with kids – although we've had three.

Mitch Murray

What is more enchanting than the voices of young people when you can't hear what they are saying?

Logan Pearsall Smith

✗ Family and Relations

I am not the boss of my house. I don't know how I lost it. I don't think I ever had it. But I've seen the boss's job and I don't want it.

Bill Cosby

The most terrible thing about children and writing is the total uncertainty of being able to plan ahead. Because the moment you sit down, they fall off a wall, they get measles.

A.S. Byatt

My daughter Olivia came in and I told her Daddy was going to play for England. She began to cry.

Lee Dixon

How can I choose a husband when I can't even decide what to wear?

Beth Jaykus

The only person who could start our lawn mower was my father and he could do this only by wrapping the rope around the starter thing, yanking it for a weekend, requiring more time and energy than if he'd cut the entire lawn with his teeth.

Dave Barry

A baby takes nine months to download.

Daniel Josipovich

You're probably a Redneck if you go Christmas shopping for your mom, sister and girlfriend and you need buy only one gift.

Jeff Foxworthy

Love, Sex, Marriage, Men and Women

A journalist once asked me if I had ever slept with a woman.
I replied that I had been accused of being many things in my
life but never of being a lesbian.

Micheal MacLiammoir

If there is anybody out there who has just bought the book
The Joy of Sex, there is a misprint on page 206.

Phyllis Diller

I don't mind my wife having the last word. In fact I'm
delighted when she reaches it.

Walter Matthau

It was not a bosom to repose upon, but it was a capital
bosom to hang jewels on.

Charles Dickens

I like you so much that sometimes it's an effort to remember
that you're a woman at all.

Terence Rattigan

Ernest Hemingway's effect upon women is such that they
want to go right out and get him and bring him home
stuffed.

Dorothy Parker

I've had so many men, the FBI come to me for fingerprints.

Mae West

My wife gives very good headache.

Rodney Dangerfield

Love, Sex, Marriage...

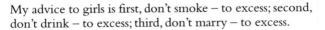

My advice to girls is first, don't smoke – to excess; second, don't drink – to excess; third, don't marry – to excess.

Mark Twain

Only time can heal a broken heart, just as only time can heal his broken arms and legs.

Miss Piggy

The closest I ever came to a menage à trois was once when I dated a schizophrenic.

Rita Rudner

The women's movement would probably be more successful if men were running it.

Jimmy Williams

Whenever you apologise to your wife the answer is always the same – 'It's too late now and it's the wrong kind of apology.'

Dave Barry

I dated this girl for two years and then the nagging started – 'Tell me your name, tell me your name.'

Mike Binder

The sock is a highly sensitive conjugal object.

Jean-Claude Kaufman

If Jack Lemmon was a homosexual, I'd marry him.

Walter Matthau

Love, Sex, Marriage...

A man is simply a woman's way of making another woman.

Samuel Butler

When I said I had sex for seven hours, that included dinner and a movie.

Phil Collins

I'm not offended by all the dumb-blonde jokes because I know I'm not dumb. I also know I'm not blonde.

Dolly Parton

A man without a woman is like a neck without a pain.

W. C. Fields

Catherine Deneuve is the man I would have liked to be.

Gerard Depardieu

Men don't understand washing machine controls because they are written in woman.

Jeremy Clarkson

I don't think my wife likes me very much. When I had a heart attack she wrote for an ambulance.

Frank Carson

I love being married. I was single for a long time and I just got sick of finishing my own sentences.

Brian Kiley

Love, Sex, Marriage...

All I have to say about men and bathrooms is that they're happy if they hit something.

Rita Rudner

I reckon it is easier to shoot your wife than to have to shoot a different man every week.

Dick Hills

I have a mirrored ceiling over my bed because I like to know what I am doing.

Mae West

O, she is the antidote to desire.

William Congreve

My husband said he needs more space. So I locked him outside.

Roseanne Barr

Greta Garbo was every man's harmless fantasy mistress. She gave you the impression that, if your imagination had to sin, it could at least congratulate itself on its impeccable taste.

Alistair Cooke

You can tell it's love, the real thing, when you dream of slitting his throat.

Wendy Cope

Every night when the moon is full a werewolf turns into a wolf – him and thirty million other guys.

Lou Costello

Most men in this town think monogamy is some kind of wood.

Mike Werb

I have chosen a very plain girlfriend – buggers can't be choosers.

Maurice Bowra

He asked me if I wanted to go back to his place. I told him I didn't know if two people could fit under a rock.

Rita Rudner

How do I feel about women's rights? Just the same way as I feel about women's lefts.

Groucho Marx

I know that blokes have feelings too – but who cares?

Jo Brand

New lovers should have a minimum isolation period of say, six months, so as not to nauseate everyone they meet.

Kathy Lette

A psychiatrist told me and my wife that we should have sex every night – now we never see each other.

Rodney Dangerfield

You get to go through 36 hours of contractions; he gets to hold your hand and say 'focus, breathe, push'.

Joan Rivers

Love, Sex, Marriage...

What's wrong with you men? Would hair stop growing on your chests if you asked directions somewhere?

Erma Bombeck

If your girlfriend wants to leave you, she should give you two weeks' notice, there should be severance pay, and before they leave, they should have to find you a temp.

Bob Ettinger

Men who have fought in the world's bloodiest wars are apt to faint at the sight of a truly foul diaper.

Gary Christenson

To intimidate your daughter's date when he picks up, let him see you sprinkling some dust on her before she leaves. Say, 'It makes fingerprinting easier.'

Mike McQueen

I think, therefore I am single.

Liz Winstead

In lovemaking, what my ex-husband lacked in size, he made up for in speed.

Roseanne Barr

The two times they pronounce you anything in life is when you are man and wife or when they pronounce you dead on arrival.

Dennis Miller

Marriage is the only legal form of pickpocketing.

> Alice Kahn

Here's a bit of advice for office managers – keep the sexual harassment complaint forms in the bottom drawer so you'll get a great view of the secretary's butt as she gets one out.

> Denis Leary

The difference between a man and a municipal bond is that municipal bonds eventually mature.

> Agnes Langer

Heidi Abromowitz has had more hands up her dress than the Muppets.

> Joan Rivers

I don't think it's a big deal that swans mate for life. If you're a swan, you're probably not going to find a swan that looks much better than the one you've got, so why not mate for life?

> Jack Handey

There ain't nothin' an ol' man can do but bring me a message from a young one.

> Moms Mabley

I'm getting old. When I squeeze into a tight parking space, I'm sexually satisfied for the day.

> Rodney Dangerfield

Love, Sex, Marriage...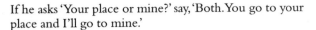

If he asks 'Your place or mine?' say, 'Both. You go to your place and I'll go to mine.'

Bette Midler

I have known and respected your husband for many years and what is good enough for him is good enough for me.

Groucho Marx

In the last stage of labour I threatened to take my husband to court for concealing a lethal weapon in his boxer shorts.

Linda Fiterman

If you love someone, set them free. If they come back, they're probably broke.

Rhonda Dickson

Women should not be enlightened or educated in any way. They should, in fact, be segregated as they are the cause of hideous and involuntary erections in holy men.

St Augustine

A control freak is any man who behaves like a woman and a nymphomaniac is any woman who behaves like a man.

Patrick Murray

I'm looking for a perfume to overpower men – I'm sick of karate.

Phyllis Diller

Love, Sex, Marriage...

My Uncle Harry was an early feminist. At a race-meeting in Ayr, he threw himself under a suffragette.

Arnold Brown

It is not good enough to spend time and ink in describing the penultimate sensations and physical movements of people getting into a state of rut, we all know them too well.

John Galsworthy

Lo, an intelligent opinion in the mouth of a woman horrifieth a man even as the scissors in the mouth of a babe.

Helen Rowland

Men wake up as good-looking as they went to bed. Women somehow deteriorate during the night.

Jerry Seinfeld

The only really firm rule of taste about cross-dressing is that neither sex should ever wear anything they haven't figured out how to go to the bathroom in.

P. J. O'Rourke

In a world without men, there would be no war – just intense negotiations every 28 days.

Robin Williams

It is my observation that women who complain of sexual harassment are, more often than not, revoltingly ugly.

Auberon Waugh

Love, Sex, Marriage...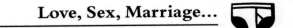

Women who insist upon having the same options as men would do well to consider the option of being the strong silent type.

Fran Lebowitz

Men are better than cats because men pee only on the carpet in the loo.

Jo Brand

My wife thinks I should buy her a new dress just because she's fed up of treading on the veil of the one she's got.

Roy Brown

The difference between a man and a battery is that a battery has a plus side.

Jo Brand

Women are like banks, boy, breaking and entering is a serious business.

Joe Orton

Monogamy is the Western custom of one wife and hardly any mistresses.

Saki

God, why didn't you make women first – when you were fresh?

Yves Montand

Love, Sex, Marriage...

In a lonely hearts advert, 'good-looking' means he's an arrogant bastard, 'huggable' means he's overweight and has got more hair than a yeti.

Mary Gold

A gold rush is what happens when a line of chorus girls spots a man with a bank roll.

Mae West

In olden times, sacrifices were made at the altar, a practice which is still very much practised.

Helen Rowland

I am never troubled by sexual desires. In fact I rather enjoy them.

Tommy Cooper

Mme de Genlis, in order to avoid the scandal of coquetry, always yielded easily.

Charles de Talleyrand

A newlywed is a guy who tells his wife when he gets a pay raise.

Leonard Levinson

If your home burns down, rescue the dogs. At least they'll be faithful to you.

Lee Marvin

It takes a lot of experience for a girl to kiss like a beginner.

Dorothy Parker

My advice is to keep two mistresses. Few men have the stamina for more.

Ovid

Sex is a subject like any other subject. Every bit as interesting as agriculture.

Muriel Spark

As a couple, they were a perfect illustration of the equation zero plus zero equals zero.

Patrick Murray

A woman is someone who can remember a hat she bought in 1938 but cannot remember what is trumps.

Joseph Soaper

My ideal man is young and handsome and looks as if his teeth will stay in all night.

Victoria Wood

Being a woman must be a great thing or otherwise so many men wouldn't be wanting to do it.

Gilda Radner

I will not meet you at the pier, my love, as it will probably be chilly.

Anton Chekhov

We ask women to do only two things – menstruate and have babies, and look at the fuss they make about both.

Scott McClue

# Love, Sex, Marriage...

Of course I've known for years our marriage has been a mockery. My body lying there night after night in the wasted moonlight. I know now how the Taj Mahal must feel.

Alan Bennett

Charles Talleyrand is in love with himself and he doesn't have a rival on earth.

Napoleon Bonaparte

A wife is a person who can look in a drawer and find her husband's socks that aren't there.

Dan Bennett

So long as spiders continue to invade our home, I can rest secure in the knowledge she daren't divorce me.

Gerry Hanson

I wanted my wife to be an economist in the kitchen and a whore in bed. She turned out to be a whore in the kitchen and an economist in bed.

Les Dawson

I like a man with an open chequebook sort of face.

Joan Rivers

A ventriloquist's dummy always seems to have a very active social and sexual life. He's always talking about dates and women that he knows and bringing them back to his suitcase at night.

Jerry Seinfeld

Love, Sex, Marriage...

Sure I'll tie the marital knot – as long as it's around her neck.

W. C. Fields

God created lesbians so that feminists can't breed.

Roy Brown

The secret of a happy marriage remains a secret.

Henny Youngman

Women over 50 cannot have babies because they would put them down and forget where they left them.

Oliver Reed

This lovely young girl said to me the other day, 'Hello, handsome, could you tell me the way to the optician's?'

Ken Dodd

A guy who would cheat on his wife would cheat at cards.

Texas Guinan

Greatest horror – I dream I am married and wake up shrieking.

J. M. Barrie

I was devastated to pick up a newspaper the other day and read that 82 per cent of British men would rather sleep with a goat than with me.

Sarah Ferguson

Love, Sex, Marriage...

I don't care what they say, women make the best wives.

Chic Young

The closest I've ever come to saying 'no' is 'not now, we're landing'.

Ted Danson

On the one hand, men never experience childbirth. On the other hand, we can open all our own jars.

Bruce Willis

'Tis better to have loved and lost than never to have lost at all.

Samuel Butler

Women may be able to fake orgasms, but men can fake whole relationships.

Sharon Stone

Of course, darling, return the ring – but keep the diamonds.

Zsa Zsa Gabor

My wife says I never listen to her. At least that's what I think she said.

Milton Berle

I discovered my wife in bed with another man and I was crushed. So I said, 'Get off me you two.'

Emo Philips

Love, Sex, Marriage...

Sex is a good thing. Someday I hope to do it again.

Jerry Seinfeld

I wanted to have a pre-nuptial agreement – not to get married.

Anne MacHale

One thing I don't understand about women – why do they have to have colour-coordinated underwear?

Robin Williams

There will always be a battle between the sexes because men and women want different things – men want women and women want men.

George Burns

My sleeping wife was snoring with all the refinement of a bronchial warthog. She sounded like the death-rattle of a moose with piles.

Les Dawson

I never kept any secrets from my wife – mind you I tried.

Mitch Murray

Fall not in love – it will stick to your face.

Dan Ackroyd

I told my father I had half a mind to get married. He said that was all I needed.

Roy Brown

Love, Sex, Marriage...

They call it a 'Pearl Wedding' because after 30 years together, you feel like stringing yourself up.

Don MacLean

One of the first signs that your wife is unhappy is when she starts lining the budgie's cage with your wedding pictures.

Roy Brown

Never do anything in bed that you can't pronounce.

Mitch Murray

Nothing confuses a man more than driving behind a woman who does everything right.

Henny Youngman

If you haven't seen a man and he hasn't called in about three weeks and if you are in doubt about his whereabouts, the chances are he is not in an emergency room moaning your name.

Diane Conway

If a 22-year-old toy boy came up to me, expressing his undying love, I would suspect his mental health.

Phyllis Diller

Now it's men who can't commit and you find 45-year-old men saying they're not ready for marriage. No, you're not, you're ready for death.

Joan Rivers

When can one love someone truly? Only when one is safely married – and then with the greatest discretion.

Oscar Wilde

I met this drop-dead gorgeous girl at a party. I said 'You're gorgeous.' She said 'Drop dead.'

Mitch Murray

I am the world's most married woman. I'm now ready to get married again – it will be marriage number 23 and it's going to last for ever. All my ex-husbands are friends with one another and I am friends with all of them.

Linda Evans

Never cry over a man. Just yell 'next'.

Denise Gilbert

I met my wife at a singles bar. We were both very surprised.

Brian Conley

How can I describe her looks? Can you imagine Yasser Arafat with plaits?

Mitch Murray

A dating agency – it's like a good bowel movement; there is an immediate elimination.

Susan Powter

Married life ain't so bad after you get so you can eat the things your wife likes.

Kin Hubbard

Love, Sex, Marriage...

Never go out with an old man. I went out with an old man one night – he gave me a love bite and left his teeth in my neck.

Joan Rivers

My wife and I have a great way of settling arguments – I admit I'm wrong and she admits she's right.

Jack Benny

Everything my wife and I do is on a 50–50 basis – I tell her what to do and she tells me where to go.

Mitch Murray

I don't give women a second thought because the first one covers everything.

Henny Youngman

We have women in the military but they don't put us in the front lines. The don't know if we can fight or if we can kill. I think we can. All the general has to do is walk over to the women and say, 'You see the enemy over there? They say you look fat in those uniforms.'

Elayne Boosler

As a 75-year-old widower, I do find it off-putting when the opposite sex stress 'own teeth and hair essential'. I would never dream of using anyone else's.

Alfred Norris

I was oversexed for only once in my life – from 1914 to 1981.

George Burns

Remember, marriage is a two-way street. I don't know what that means, but remember it.

George Burns

All honeymooners should hire a third party to ease the conversation during that most difficult time.

Robert Morley

The material for my book *A Guide to Men* was collected directly from nature at great personal risk by the author.

Helen Rowland

The main trouble with women is that they never put the toilet seat back up.

Martin Clunes

A man's heart may have a secret sanctuary where only one woman may enter, but it is full of little anterooms which are seldom vacant.

Helen Rowland

Marriage is a wonderful institution. If it weren't for marriage, husbands and wives would have to fight with total strangers.

Patrick Murray

He took his misfortune like a man – he blamed it on his wife.

Bob Phillips

Love, Sex, Marriage...

For novelty in your sex life, both partners should sit in the cupboard under the stairs and try to identify parts of the gas meter and vacuum cleaner by touch.

Mark Leigh

If there were no husbands, who would look after our mistresses?

George Moore

It is better to have loved even your wife than never to have loved at all.

Edgar Saltus

You must have women dressed, if it is only for the pleasure of imagining them as Venuses.

George Moore

It's our story exactly! He bold as a hawk, she soft as the dawn.

James Thurber

Every decision a woman makes is right.

Germaine Greer

Media and Films

Media and Films

Clifford Makins was a legend in his own lunchtime.

Christopher Wordsworth

And here they are, Jayne Mansfield.

Jack Parr

Hillary Clinton could not pose nude in *Penthouse* because they don't have a page that broad.

Gennifer Flowers

Ask about our cup size or favourite position, but please – no personal questions.

Shane Barbi

If I've still got my pants on in the second scene, I think they've sent me the wrong script.

Mel Gibson

A new study reveals that guests on daytime talk shows are predominantly female. Of course most of them weren't born that way.

Conan O'Brien

Groucho Marx had the compassion of an icicle and the generosity of a pawnbroker.

S. J. Perelman

The 'g' in Camille Paglia's name is silent – about the only part of her that is.

Julie Burchill

Media and Films

My interest in the cinema has lapsed since women began to talk.

George J. Nathan

Making a film with Greta Garbo does not constitute an introduction.

Robert Montgomery

Jack Warner never bore a grudge against anyone he wronged.

Simone Signoret

Mr Myers misjudged the mood of the *Late Late Show* and went down like a cupful of warm Dettol with a hair in it.

Hugh Leonard

The right side of Claudette Colbert's face was called the other side of the moon because nobody ever saw it.

Mary Astor

When you want a man to play with you, wear a full-length black nightgown with buttons all over it. Sure it's uncomfortable, but it makes you look like his remote control.

Joan Rivers

Gilbert Harding was a take-away Dr Johnson.

John Osborne

Media and Films

I am too short to play Oscar Wilde – except on radio, the last refuge of the physically disqualified.

Simon Callow

The biggest prize we ever gave away on *Blankety Blank* was a weekend in Reykjavik.

Terry Wogan

Working with the Marx Brothers was not unlike being chained to a galleycar and lashed at ten-minute intervals.

S. J. Perelman

Quality newspaper journalism – interdepartmental memoranda for the elite.

A. J. P. Taylor

Giving your book to Hollywood is like turning your daughter over to a pimp.

Tom Clancy

If I had my life to live over I would do everything the exact same way – with the possible exception of seeing the movie remake of *Lost Horizon*.

Woody Allen

Nobody likes my acting except the public.

John Wayne

They are doing things on the screen now that the French don't even put on postcards.

Bob Hope

Media and Films

The invention of television can be compared to the introduction of indoor plumbing. Fundamentally it brought no change in the public's habits. It simply eliminated the necessity of leaving the house.

Alfred Hitchcock

I give hope to the hopeless. People look at me and say: 'If he can make it, I can be Queen of England.'

Robert Mitchum

Clark Gable – the best ears of our lives.

Milton Berle

I am the Ukrainian Cary Grant.

Walter Matthau

It is true that I am a low mean snake. But Ted Turner could walk beneath me wearing a top hat.

Rupert Murdoch

Then came *Easy Rider*, a disaster in the history of film to set beside the loss of Technicolour, the early death of Murnau, and the longevity of Richard Attenborough.

David Thomson

One of my pictures was so bad, they had to do retakes before they threw it in the bin.

King Vidor

Elizabeth Taylor has an unlisted dress size.

Joan Rivers

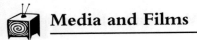

John Ford was a son of a bitch who also happened to be a genius.

Henry Fonda

As a simple reporter I decided that facts must never get in the way of the truth.

James Cameron

Rudolph Valentino had the acting talents of the average wardrobe.

Clyde Jeavons

I kept the same suit for six years – and the same dialogue. We just changed the title of the picture and the leading lady.

Robert Mitchum

Anyone who leaves De Mille for the armed forces is a coward.

Charlton Heston

Bad reviews of my pictures run off my back like a duck.

Samuel Goldwyn

In Ben Hur, Charlton Heston throws all his punches in the first ten minutes (three grimaces and two intonations) so that he has nothing left long before he stumbles to the end, four hours later, and has to react to the crucifixion. (He does make it clear, I must admit, that he disapproves of it.)

Dwight MacDonald

Media and Films

Some of my best leading men have been horses and dogs.

Elizabeth Taylor

You can quote me as saying that I was misquoted.

Groucho Marx

Camelot is the Platonic idea of boredom roughly comparable to reading a three-volume novel in a language of which one knows only the alphabet.

John Simon

I sometimes think I shall never view
A French film lacking Gerard Depardieu

John Updike

People think I have an interesting walk. Hell, I'm just trying to hold my gut in.

Robert Mitchum

Go into any major studio and shout 'Fill her up', and all the leading men in the place will instinctively come running.

Humphrey Bogart

Men don't care what's on TV. They only care what else is on TV.

Jerry Seinfeld

The other night I saw a *Road* picture on TV so cut to make room for 45 commercials that Bing and I weren't even in it.

Bob Hope

I was pretty – so pretty that actresses didn't want to work with me.

Roger Moore

Fred Astaire is the closest we are ever likely to get to a human Mickey Mouse.

Graham Greene

Did you know that the historic figures John Calvin and Thomas Hobbes were named after popular comic strip characters?

Paul Johnston

Billy Wilder at work is two people – Mr Hyde and Mr Hyde.

Harry Kurnitz

The making of a journalist: no ideas and the ability to express them.

Karl Kraus

My wife doesn't get jealous when she sees me in sex scenes on the screen. She knows I am only acting and that I can't last that long.

Jeremy Irons

Raise the Titanic? It would have been cheaper to lower the Atlantic.

Lew Grade

Media and Films

To have Mae Marsh display a surprised look, D. W. Griffith had a gun discharged behind her back. The effect lasted fifty years.

James Agate

The talkies made me sound as if I had been castrated.

Tallulah Bankhead

It's simple. PG means the hero gets the girl, 15 means that the villain gets the girl and 18 means that everybody gets the girl.

Michael Douglas

Star Spangled Rhythm is a variety show including everyone at Paramount who was not overseas, in hiding or out to lunch.

James Agee

Gary Cooper was one of the best loved illiterates this country has ever known.

Carl Sandburg

Many a good story has been ruined by over-verification.

James Bennett

On radio every Sunday, we have a stroke of culture, a symphony concert from New York or somewhere with a tooth-wash. That's the culture part, the tooth-wash.

Lincoln Steffens

Media and Films

When I first saw my future husband Jim Threapleton, then just a third assistant director, I thought to myself 'I'm not going to get through this with my legs crossed.'

Kate Winslet

Collaboration – that's the word producers use. That means, don't forget to kiss my ass from beginning to end.

Sam Shepard

My wife listens only to Radio Four. It could run a two-hour shipping forecast and she would not retune to another station.

Jeremy Clarkson

I believe in equality for everyone, except reporters and photographers.

Mahatma Gandhi

I've been asked where I'm going to shoot *The Horse Soldiers*. I think I'll shoot it in Lourdes because it's going to take a miracle to make anything of it.

John Ford

Night watchmen in horror movies have a life expectancy of twelve seconds.

Sam Waas

Tell the actors to stand closer apart.

Samuel Goldwyn

Media and Films

In this business we make movies, American movies. Leave the films to the French.

Sam Shepard

Radio One is out, unless you enjoy being serenaded by people banging bits of furniture together. Radio Three transmits nothing but the sound of small animals being tortured.

Jeremy Clarkson

His ambition was to be a bouncer on the Jerry Springer Show but he failed the intelligence test.

Patrick Murray

I've had several years in Hollywood and I still think the real movie heroes are in the audience.

Wilson Mizner

If you watch the credits of any movie to the very end you will see at least one person listed who has the same last name as the director or one of the producers.

David Burd

Bette Davis — take away the pop eyes, the cigarettes and those funny clipped words and what have you got?

Joan Crawford

Jayne Mansfield is Miss United Dairies herself.

David Niven

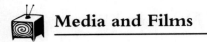 **Media and Films**

Film-making has become a kind of hysterical pregnancy.

Richard Lester

I think it's so quaint that Estelle Winwood is making a whole new career of merely being very old. I hope I never live so long that I get hired simply for not being a corpse.

Elsa Lanchester

Life is difficult enough without Meryl Streep movies.

Truman Capote

My friends thought the movie stank but I can't say I like it that much.

James Thurber

A reporter is something between a whore and a bartender.

Wallace Smith

Nothing difficult is ever easy.

Yogi Berra

Fox may not make good films but it leads the world in landscape gardening.

Eric Knight

Louis Theroux went in search of the perfectly formed Paul Daniels and his other half from the weather-vane house, Debbie McGee.

A.A. Gill

Media and Films

Glenda Jackson is the thinking man's Hilda Ogden.

Henry Root

I don't care what's written about me so long as it isn't true.

Dorothy Parker

George Raft is an actor, who, when he gets all dressed up, looks like a stolen car.

Orson Bean

I vow to spend the rest of my life shaming the press into upholding its moral obligations.

Bill Clinton

I love Shirley MacLaine dearly, but her oars aren't touching the water these days.

Dean Martin

The main competition for the book is the video because people feel they need to come home with a rectangular block of something that they don't know the end of.

Jerry Seinfeld

Hampden Park is the only ground which looks the same in black and white as it does in colour.

David Lacey

The world looks a totally different place after two wins. I can even enjoy watching *Blind Date* or laugh at *Noel's House Party*.

Gordon Strachan

Move those ten thousand horses a trifle to the right. And that mob there, three feet forward.

D. W. Griffith

There were so many stories about the Royal Family, it was almost inevitable some of them would turn out to be true.

Nigel Evans

When in doubt, make a Western.

John Ford

The lowest depth to which people can sink before God is defined by the word 'journalist'.

Soren Kierkegaard

Geri Halliwell shocked TV viewers the other day when she spelled out a four-letter word – correctly.

Frank Skinner

Theatre is life. Film is art. Television is furniture.

Scott Adams

The action replay showed it was worse than it actually was.

Ron Atkinson

It's amazing that the amount of news that happens in the world every day always just exactly fits the newspaper.

Jerry Seinfeld

Media and Films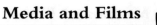

I am 46 and have been for some time past.

Anita Brookner

I once thought of becoming a political cartoonist because they have to come up with only one idea a day. Then I thought I'd become a sportswriter instead because they don't have to come up with any.

Sam Snead

Before you decide to retire, stay home for a week and watch the daytime TV shows.

Bill Copeland

If you ever see me being beaten by the police, put down that video camera and come and help me.

Bobcat Goldtwait

How did I shoot that scene? With a camera.

John Ford

David Frost rose without trace.

Kitty Muggeridge

Making a picture with Marilyn Monroe was like a visit to the dentist. It was hell at the time, but after it was all over, it was wonderful.

Billy Wilder

Carrying a camcorder always makes me feel as if I had been artificially inseminated with a supermarket trolley.

Alan Davies

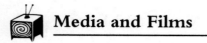

I'm not a real movie star. I've still got the same wife I started out with 28 years ago.

Will Rogers

The key to a successful marriage in Hollywood is separate houses. Living on separate coasts is even better, like New York and LA – those bicoastal marriages work well. Separate countries is best of all.

Kelly Lange

He was over to the poorhouse the other day to see an old friend that used to publish a newspaper that pleased everybody.

Kin Hubbard

In Hollywood there is a simple equation to explain the constant flirtation between actors and politicians: actors know that everybody likes them but nobody takes them seriously; politicians know that everybody takes them seriously but nobody likes them.

James Bone

Except for the Flood, nothing was ever as bad as reported.

E. W. Howe

American comedies are as funny as a baby with cancer.

Spike Milligan

All they ever did for me at MGM was to change my leading men and the water in the pool.

Esther Williams

Media and Films

The name of Ursula Andress has always seemed a Spoonerism to me.

John Simon

Monogamy does exist in Hollywood, but it would be a lot more popular if it didn't sound so much like monotony.

Rita Rudner

Clark Gable has enemies all right – but they all like him.

David Selznick

When I was invited to leave my impression in the cement at Hollywood, it was suggested that instead of using my hands or my feet I should use my most outstanding features instead; but I was afraid some little kid might fall in and get hurt.

Dolly Parton

A film musician is like a mortician – he can't bring the body back to life, but he's expected to make it look better.

Adolph Deutsch

Goodbye, Mr Zanuck: it certainly has been a pleasure working at 16th Century Fox.

Jean Renoir

Normally in a movie I'm in love with truth, Richard Burton or a camel.

Peter O'Toole

I was promised the tallest, darkest leading man in Hollywood and I got him – King Kong.

Fay Wray

I have received no more than one or two letters in my life that were worth the postage.

Henry David Thoreau

James Dean dead? How could he do this to me after all my work to build him up into a big star?

Jack Warner

Yes, I did appear in the Sound of Mucus.

Christopher Plummer

The match will be shown on *Match of the Day* this evening. If you don't want to know the result, look away now as we show you Tony Adams lifting up the cup for Arsenal.

Steve Rider

Miss Garland's figure resembles the giant economy-size tube of toothpaste found in girls' bathrooms: squeezed intemperately at all points it acquires a shape that defies definition by the most resourceful solid geometer.

John Simon

I think anyone responsible for depicting violence on television should be kicked in the head, have his eyes gouged, his nose chopped off, be run through with a sword, and shot in the left hip.

Gregory McDonald

There are days when any electrical appliance in the house, including the vacuum cleaner, seems to offer more entertainment possibilities than the TV set.

Harriet Van Horne

The most beautiful words in journalism are 'A. A. Gill is away.'

Ronald White

Adapting *Middlemarch* for TV was like getting an elephant into a suitcase.

Andrew Davis

After a film has been edited, the producer holds a private screening for fifty of his friends. It's called a screening because he screens out anyone who might give an honest opinion of his movie.

George Burns

Dancing at Lughnasa was widely ignored by audiences and savaged by critics, much like Meryl Streep's baby was in *A Cry in the Dark*.

Sian O'Gorman

Last year, the White House complained to Hollywood that there was too much sex in the movies.

Billy Crystal

In institutions people weave baskets — busy fingers are happy fingers — I make films.

Woody Allen

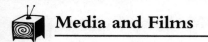# Media and Films

Early to bed and early to rise is a sure sign you're fed up with TV.

Bob Phillips

I knew Dolly Parton when she was wearing a trainer bra.

George Burns

Medicine and Doctors

Medicine and Doctors

I've just got the bill for my operation. Now I know why those guys were wearing masks.

Jim Boren

I have a friend who died from a simple sneeze. Of course, he was standing in his neighbour's bedroom closet at the time.

Charles Jarvis

When I prepare to go to sleep, everything comes off or out.

Phyllis Diller

I think my kid is going to be a doctor. Nobody can read anything he writes.

Henny Youngman

My mother had morning sickness after I was born.

Rodney Dangerfield

My wife lost two stones swimming last year. I don't know how. I tied them around her neck tight enough.

Les Dawson

When the doctor asked me if I became breathless when taking exercise, I had to say no, as I never took exercise.

John Mortimer

I have been on a convalescent diet. If you come across nineteen or eighteen pounds of human flesh, they belong to me. I look as if a curate has been taken out of me.

Sydney Smith

Medicine and Doctors

I've examined your son's head, Mr Glum, and there's nothing there.

Frank Muir

Does your epileptic fit, or do you have to take him in a bit at the sides?

Jason Byrne

The placenta is very useful because it is so very hideous that by comparison, the baby is quite attractive.

Jenny Eclair

In some ways, cramp is worse than having a broken leg. But leukaemia is worse still. Probably.

Kevin Keegan

When I was pregnant my breasts were so huge they needed their own postcode.

Kathy Lette

During one of his many bouts of insanity King George the Third insisted on ending every sentence with the word 'peacock'.

Geoff Tibballs

Nancy Reagan has agreed to be the first artificial heart donor.

Andrea Michaels

No man is a hero to his wife's psychiatrist.

Eric Berne

Medicine and Doctors

I had examined myself pretty thoroughly and discovered that I was unfit for military service.

Joseph Heller

Nothing is dearer to a woman than a nice long obstetrical chat.

Cornelia Otis Skinner

I went to the doctor the other day and told him my arm was broken in three places. He told me to stay out of those places.

Tommy Cooper

They say men can never experience the pain of childbirth; they can if you hit them in the goolies with a cricket bat for fourteen hours.

Jo Brand

A cough is something that you yourself can't help, but everybody else does on purpose just to torment you.

Ogden Nash

He cured his sciatica by boiling his buttock.

John Aubrey

My friend George is weird. He has false teeth – with braces on them.

Steven Wright

Medicine and Doctors

A natural death is where you die by yourself without the aid of a doctor.

Mark Twain

I went to the doctor and he told me I had acute paranoia. I reminded him that I had come to be examined, not to be admired.

Gracie Allen

Physicians of all men are most happy; what good success soever they have, the world proclaimeth and what faults they commit the earth covereth.

Francis Quarles

The first need in the reform of hospital management is the death of all dietitians and the resurrection of the French chef.

Martin Fischer

I'm not saying my body is a wreck, but my gynaecologist wears a hard hat.

Joan Rivers

The doctor told me I should buy day-returns from now on instead of season tickets.

Hugh Leonard

It is a known medical fact, and it has been so since the dawn of time, that a man asking directions will hear just the first word and then break down.

Jeremy Clarkson

Medicine and Doctors

It is better to be dead, or even perfectly well, than to suffer from the wrong affliction. The man who owns up to arthritis in beriberi year is as lonely as a woman in a last month's dress.

Ogden Nash

The doctors were very brave about my illness.

Dorothy Parker

I have Bright's disease and he has mine.

S. J. Perelman

Keep up the spirits of your patient with the music of the viol and the psaltery, or by forging letters telling of the death of his enemies or (if he be a cleric) by informing him that he has been made a bishop.

Henri De Mondeville

I do not in any way approve of the modern sympathy with invalids. I consider it morbid. Illness of any kind is hardly a thing to be encouraged in others.

Oscar Wilde

His condition is improving rapidly – he is sitting up in bed blowing the froth off his medicine.

Flann O'Brien

Mr Anaesthetist, if the patient can stay awake, surely you can.

Wilfred Trotter

Medicine and Doctors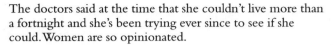

The doctors said at the time that she couldn't live more than a fortnight and she's been trying ever since to see if she could. Women are so opinionated.

Saki

I stuck my head out the window and got arrested for mooning.

Rodney Dangerfield

The reason we cannot read a doctor's prescription is because they all carry the same message to the pharmacist – 'I got my money, now get yours.'

Jackie Mason

Free your mind and your bottom will follow.

Sarah Ferguson

My dear old friend, King George the Fifth, always told me that he would never have died but for that vile doctor, Lord Dawson of Penn.

Margot Asquith

Peter Swales loves publicity. He wears a card round his neck saying 'In case of a heart attack, call a press conference.'

Tommy Docherty

'Gentle' is a lovely word used to describe the action of a laxative.

William Feather

Suicide is cheating the doctors out of a job.

Josh Billings

I'm in pretty good shape for the shape I'm in.

Mickey Rooney

There is many a man who would be glad to get up out of his grave and cough.

Antoine Condon

I've never had amnesia – not that I can remember anyway.

Dominic MacHale

Where do you go to get anorexia?

Shelley Winters

A Florida woman is suing her doctor after she ended up with four breasts following cosmetic surgery. Her surgeon, she later discovered, was an ear, nose and throat specialist.

Jaci Stephen

Seven out of every ten people suffer from piles. Does that mean the other three enjoy them?

Sal Davino

By the way, my brother says hello. So hooray for speech therapy.

Emo Philips

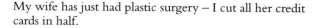

My wife has just had plastic surgery – I cut all her credit cards in half.

Roy Brown

When a man gets to 30, so does his body.

Glenn Hoddle

My doctor forbids me to play unless I win.

Alexander Woollcott

There are two reasons to sit in the back row of an aeroplane: either you have diarrhoea, or you're anxious to meet a lot of people who do.

Henry Kissinger

I am in shape. Round is a shape.

Roseanne Barr

I have never knowingly bitten another player. For one thing I believe in good hygiene.

Conrad Dobler

Paranoids are people too; they have their own problems. It's easy to criticise, but if everybody hated you, you'd be paranoid too.

D. J. Hicks

The older you get the tougher it is to lose weight because by then your body and your fat are really good friends.

Roseanne Barr

Medicine and Doctors

Happiness is your dentist saying it won't hurt, and then having him catch his hand in the drill.

Peter O'Donovan

Isn't it a bit unnerving that doctors call what they do 'practice'?

George Carlin

I may be fat but you're ugly – and I can lose weight.

Jo Brand

Health consists of having the same diseases as one's neighbours.

Quentin Crisp

My left foot is not one of my best.

Sammy McIlroy

I don't have anything against face-lifts, but I think a good rule of thumb is that it's time to stop when you look permanently frightened.

Susan Forfleet

All my clothes are made from natural fibres but my breasts are man-made.

Nora Dunn

Asthma doesn't seem to bother me unless I'm around cigars or dogs. The thing that would bother me most would be a dog smoking a cigar.

Steve Allen

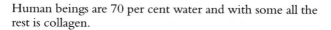

Human beings are 70 per cent water and with some all the rest is collagen.

Martin Mull

The only thing that can be guaranteed to stop falling hair is the floor.

Will Rogers

Demi Moore has had plastic surgery on everything except her toes and they're next on the list.

Malcolm Levene

The diaphragm is a muscular partition separating disorders of the chest from disorders of the bowels.

Ambrose Bierce

Some people are so sensitive that they feel snubbed if an epidemic overlooks them.

Kin Hubbard

If you've never suffered from insomnia, you cannot know what a nightmare it is.

Karen Keating

There's a sort of decency among the dead, a remarkable discretion: you never find them making any complaint against the doctor who killed them.

Molière

Medicine and Doctors

A hundred years ago there were no bacilli, no ptomaine poisoning, no diphtheria, and no appendicitis. Rabies was but little known, and only imperfectly developed. All of these we owe to medical science. Even such things as parotitus and psoriasis, which are now household names, were known only to the few, and were quite beyond the reach of the great mass of people.

Stephen Leacock

Pantagruel thought of studying medicine but decided the profession was too troublesome and morbid. Besides, physicians smelled hellishly of enemas.

François Rabelais

If you are going to have a heart attack, one of the best places to have it is on the course of the marathon because there are so many medics to hand.

Nick Bitel

Death is what some patients do merely to humiliate the doctor.

Voltaire

In psychiatry it is not a good idea to place a person who hears voices next to a person who mumbles to himself.

Lily Tomlin

The difference between the psychiatrists and the patients at a mental hospital is that the patients eventually get better and go home.

Alex Tan

Medicine and Doctors

In Hollywood if you don't have a psychiatrist, people think you're crazy.

Bob Hope

A proctologist is a doctor who starts out at the bottom and stays there.

Joe Tierney

The nurse who can smile when things go wrong is probably going off duty.

Derek Cashman

I knew this homoeopath who forgot to take his medicine and died of an overdose.

Steven Wright

The doctor told me my condition was so rare, they weren't even sure if they were pronouncing it correctly.

Morey Armstrong

The Secretary of State for Health died this morning. Doctors said his condition was satisfactory.

Kenneth Clarke

Music

 **Music**

Being music director of the Berlin Philharmonic is like being the Pope – except for the celibacy.

Simon Rattle

I've just been listening to a sonata written by Chopin in a flat; you'd think with the sort of money he was earning he could afford a house.

Alastair McGowan

Michael Jackson started life as a black boy; now he's a white girl.

Mary Connelly

The opera always loses money. That's as it should be. Opera has no business making money.

Rudolf Bing

We live in a country where John Lennon takes six bullets to the chest. Yoko Ono is standing next to him. Not one ******* bullet. Explain that to me! Explain that to me.

Denis Leary

Movie music is noise. It's more painful than even my sciatica.

Thomas Beecham

The soloist tonight reminded me very much of Paderewski. Paderewski was no violinist, and neither was the soloist tonight.

George Bernard Shaw

Bing Crosby sings like everybody thinks they sing in the shower.

Dinah Shore

Lionel Bart's musical *Blitz* was very close to the real thing but it seemed to last twice as long and be just as noisy.

Noël Coward

I would have given my right arm to be a pianist.

Bobby Robson

Greig's music is like a pink bon-bon filled with snow.

Claude Debussy

In the Sixties I played lead guitar in a band called the Federal Duck and we made an album which sounds like a group of people who have been given powerful but unfamiliar instruments as a therapy for a degenerative nerve disease.

Dave Barry

A musical is a series of catastrophes ending with a floor show.

Oscar Levant

It was the most fun I've had since I've been black.

Dizzy Gillespie

I know the acoustics in the hall are terrible. But we've done everything to remedy the situation – we've put down traps, we've put down poison and we still can't shift them.

Jon Kenny

Music

Last night I played a blank tape at full blast. The mime living next door went nuts.

Steven Wright

If Yoko Ono's singing voice was a fight, they'd stop it.

Robert Wuhl

Mick Jagger told me his wrinkles were due to laughter and not age. I told him that nothing was that funny.

George Melly

For the score of a movie, I like music like Wagner, only louder.

Samuel Goldwyn

Most bands don't think about the future. Most musicians can't even spell future. Lunch is how far we think ahead.

David Roth

The problem with reality is the lack of background music.

Steven Wright

Mozart composed symphonies at eight, but they weren't very good.

Steven Pinker

The people of Halifax invented the harmonium, a device for castrating pigs during the Sunday service.

Mike Harding

Can she sing? Why, she's practically a Florence Nightingale.

Samuel Goldwyn

I do not accept floral wreaths at the end of a performance. Floral wreaths are for prima donnas or corpses. I am neither.

Arturo Toscanini

I don't normally sing and when I sing I don't sing normally.

Danny Cummins

Chopin was a composer for the right hand.

Richard Wagner

My address? I think 'Italy' will be sufficient.

Giuseppe Verdi

I have heard Liszt and I have heard Paderewski, but neither of them perspired as much as Liebling does.

W. S. Gilbert

Leonard Bernstein is an educator who has been disclosing musical secrets which have been well-known for years.

Oscar Levant

A quartet is a singing group in which all four think the other three cannot sing.

Doris Maloney

 **Music**

The triumphs of Tom Jones in singles like 'It's Not Unusual' and 'Delilah' have earned him a permanent niche in the annals of nursing-home rock.

John Swenson

I've never really understood the importance of the orchestra conductor. I mean between you and me, what the hell is this guy doing? Do you really need somebody waving a stick in your face to play the violin?

Jerry Seinfeld

Who would I recommend to set *Pygmalion* to music? Mozart.

George Bernard Shaw

It's called rap music because the 'c' fell off the printer.

Allan Pease

I've had my voice trained – they put newspapers down under me.

Ken Dodd

If a musician comes to your door, pay him and take your pizza.

Zig Ziglar

La Donna Mobile – does anyone want to buy a lady's bike?

Ken Dodd

I love to sing and to drink Scotch. Most people would prefer to hear me drinking Scotch.

George Burns

I met Mick Jagger when I was playing for Oxford United and the Rolling Stones played a concert there. Little did I know that one day he'd be almost as famous as me.

Ron Atkinson

When she sang, he sat like one entranced. She touched his organ, and from that bright epoch, even it, the old companion of his happiest hours, incapable as he had thought of elevation, began a new and deified existence.

Charles Dickens

A phonograph is an irritating toy that restores life to dead noises.

Ambrose Bierce

When buying a used car, punch the buttons on the radio. If all the stations are rock and roll, there's a good chance the transmission is shot.

Larry Lujac

The 'Red Flag' sounds like the funeral march of a fried eel.

George Bernard Shaw

 **Music**

In Chiari's 'Per Arco', a cellist sits slumped like a spastic moron, over his instrument and during some 15 minutes does nothing but make an unsuccessful attempt to draw his bow across the strings of his instrument. This work was described by an admirer as 'tragic'.

Peter Heyworth

George Formby recorded nearly two hundred songs. The weary music-lover might sigh that there is only one tune, and the sensitive librettist claim that there is only one lyric.

Eric Midwinter

Terrible news – Des O'Connor has just made an unbreakable record.

Ernie Wise

When Max Bygraves played Jersey, the residents there said that if it came to a toss-up, they'd rather have the Germans back.

Bernard Manning

Love is like a set of bagpipes – you never know what to do with your hands.

Ken Dodd

John Lennon would have had his 56th birthday today. I wonder how old would he be if he was alive?

Paula White

Of course, Bizet never knew that *Carmen* was a great success until after his death.

Michael Barclay

I cannot change the world – I am not a folk singer.

Rich Hall

There's just nothing like a hardship song to set your toes a-tappin'.

Roseanne Barr

I am completely exhausted from too much wine, women and song, so I seriously contemplating giving up singing.

Henny Youngman

Critics are drooling, drivelling, doleful, depressing, dropsical drips.

Thomas Beecham

We conductors live so long because we perspire so much.

John Barbirolli

Who was that oboe I saw you with last night? That was no oboe, that was my fife.

Groucho Marx

It got to the point where I had to get a haircut or a violin.

Franklin Roosevelt

I am incapable of a tune. I have been practising 'God Save the King' all my life, whistling and humming it over to myself in solitary corners; and am not yet arrived, they tell me, within many quavers of it.

Charles Lamb

Music

People applaud a prima donna as they do the feats of the strong man at the fair. The sensations are painfully disagreeable, hard to endure, but one is so glad when it is all over that one cannot help rejoicing.

Jean-Jacques Rousseau

The banging and slamming and booming and crashing of *Lohengrin* were something beyond belief. The racking and pitiless pain of it remain stored up in my memory alongside the memory of the time I had my teeth fixed.

Mark Twain

The Prelude to Wagner's *Tristan and Isolde* reminds me of the Old Italian painting of a martyr whose intestines are slowly unwound from his body on a reel.

Eduard Hanslick

I never touched Elvis's money. He got his half.

Tom Parker

Our music group has been asked to perform at a Mass for the Catholic Deaf Association. What should we make of such an invitation? Should we be delighted or dismayed?

Angela Minoli

The function of rock'n'roll is to annoy parents.

Bob Merlis

I don't know what real childbirth is like, but writing songs seems as close as I'm going to come.

Billy Joel

The smartest thing I ever heard anybody say in rock'n'roll was 'Be-bop-a-lila, she's my baby.'

Paul Simon

How wonderful opera would be if there were no singers.

Gioachino Rossini

The difference between a bagpipe and an onion is that nobody cries when you chop up a bagpipe.

Henry Quelp

There is a new classical music group consisting of two dogs and a cat. They call themselves Bark, Oftenbark and Depussy.

Marie Jones

Nationalities and Places

Nationalities and Places

In Yorkshire folk will occasionally smile, usually when they are about to pass wind.

Simon Henry

In the Romanian army no one beneath the rank of major is permitted to wear lipstick.

Evelyn Waugh

In all my long experience as Her Majesty's hangman only one of my customers ever put up a struggle – and he wasn't British.

Albert Pierrepoint

My birthplace was near the monkey cage in Regent's Park Zoo – it was pure luck I was outside the cage.

Donald McGill

The Americans have a proud and noble tradition of being utterly hopeless in warfare. They lost in Vietnam, they lost in Somalia, they lost in the Bay of Pigs and though they won the Gulf War, they managed to kill more British soldiers than the Iraqis.

Jeremy Clarkson

People say to me things like 'You're Irish – you must be stupid.' I'm stumped.

Jimeoin McKeown

American men seem to be interested in only two things – money and breasts.

Hedy Lamarr

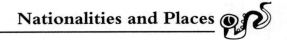

The difference between a French kiss and a Belgian kiss is that a Belgian kiss is half Flemish.

Roy Mason

I don't despair about the cultural scene in Australia because there isn't one here to despair about.

Robert Helpman

French films follow a basic formula: husband sleeps with Jeanne because Bernadette cuckolded him by sleeping with Christophe, and in the end they all go off to a restaurant.

Sophie Marceau

In England only uneducated people show off their knowledge; nobody quotes Latin or Greek authors in the course of conversation, unless he has never read them.

George Mikes

I love Morocco – it's a combination of the Bible and Hollywood.

George Patton

I was once criticised for swearing on television. The word I used was 'bloody' which, where I come from in Yorkshire, is practically the only surviving adjective.

Maureen Lipman

If you ever see two people on a boat on the Clyde in Glasgow, you know one of them is not coming back.

Danny Bhoy

There's an Ethiopian in the fuel supply.

> W. C. Fields

I have recently been all round the world and have formed a very poor opinion of it.

> Thomas Beecham

The shortest way out of Manchester is notoriously a bottle of Gordon's gin.

> William Bolitho

As a means of shortening your life-span I heartily recommend London.

> Kingsley Amis

We produced *Brigadoon* on the MGM lot because I went to Scotland and found nothing there that looked like Scotland.

> Arthur Freed

The Italian flag is a white cross on a white background.

> P. J. O'Rourke

You know you are Canadian when you know which leaves make good toilet paper.

> Heather Turnbull

In a museum in Havana there are two skulls of Christopher Columbus – one when he was a boy and one when he was a man.

> Mark Twain

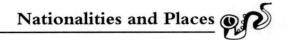

Denial ain't just a river in Egypt.

Mark Twain

Los Angeles is where you've got to go to be an actor. You go there or New York. I flipped a coin – it came up New York. So I flipped it again.

Harrison Ford

It is because of their sins and more particularly the wicked and detestable vice of homosexuality, that the Welsh were punished by God and so first lost Troy and then Britain.

Girald DeBarri

Please God, let there be victory – before the Americans arrive.

Douglas Haig

For years the Soviet Union has stood on the edge of an abyss. Now, fellow countrymen, we must take a great step forward.

Boris Yeltsin

Where I grew up in Brooklyn, nobody committed suicide. Everyone was too unhappy.

Woody Allen

At birth when a Welshman is slapped on the behind, he does not cry; he sings Men of Harlech in perfect pitch.

Alan Jay Lerner

Tourists – have some fun with New York's cabbies. When you get to your destination, say to your driver, 'Pay? I was only hitchhiking.'

Dave Letterman

Anytime four New Yorkers get into a cab together without arguing, a bank robbery has just taken place.

Johnny Carson

We should have the Queen for reigning, the Duke of Edinburgh for putting his foot in it, Prince Charles for pursuing his eccentric hobbyhorses, Prince William for waiting in the wings, and the Queen Mother for waving from balconies. That's enough Royals.

Keith Waterhouse

In Canada we have enough to do keeping up with two spoken languages without trying to invent slang, so we just go right ahead and use English for literature, Scotch for sermons and American for conversations.

Stephen Leacock

I would not however, push the case for a sense of history quite so far as the History Fellow of an Oxford College who criticised the reasoning behind the Bursar's investment policy on the grounds that the last two hundred years had been exceptional.

Donald MacDougall

Nationalities and Places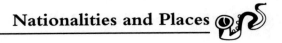

In England you will find people so desirous of titles that, if they cannot acquire them, they will stick two surnames together with a hyphen.

Oliver St John Gogarty

The shortage of parking spaces in Boston is like an alcatraz around my neck.

Thomas Menino

My favourite British weather forecast, culled from a newspaper, reads in toto, 'Dry and warm, but cooler with some rain.'

Bill Bryson

The only idea of wit that the Scots have is laughing immoderately at stated intervals.

Sydney Smith

The American GIs are overpaid, overfed, oversexed and over here.

Tommy Trinder

Nothing is more narrow-minded than chauvinism or race hatred. To me all men are equal; they are jackasses everywhere and I have the same contempt for all. No petty prejudices.

Karl Kraus

Rome is a very loony city in every respect. One needs to spend only an hour or two there to realise that Fellini made documentaries.

Fran Lebowitz

Nationalities and Places

What depresses me about this country is the way more and more money is being given to the working classes to spend on their unpleasant enthusiasms, such as transistor radios, sweets, caravans, frozen food, plastic flowers, souvenir spoons from dreadful places, which can only make England a nastier country.

Auberon Waugh

I know of only four languages – Latin, Irish, Greek and Chinese. These are languages because they are instruments of integral civilisation. English and French are not languages: they are mercantile codes.

Flann O'Brien

The British national anthem belongs to the eighteenth century. In it you find us ordering God about to do our political work.

George Bernard Shaw

In Chicago not only your vote counts, but all kinds of other votes – kids, dead folks and so on.

Dick Gregory

Any multimillionaire can grow up to become President of the United States.

Richard Wallis

To Naples for a few days, for a bracing glimpse of the poor.

Auberon Waugh

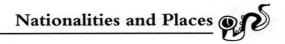

A Scotchman must be a very sturdy moralist who does not love Scotland more than the truth.

Samuel Johnson

I wouldn't mind seeing China if I could come back the same night. I hate being abroad.

Philip Larkin

Very little is known of the Canadian country since it is rarely visited by anyone but the Queen and illiterate sports fishermen.

P. J. O'Rourke

'We must have lunch sometime,' in the hypocritical code of English manners means, 'I do not care if I ever see you again.'

Philip Howard

Manhattan is a narrow island off the coast of New Jersey devoted to the pursuit of lunch.

Raymond Sokolov

In Spain a society for the protection of animals was once founded but they were short of money. So they put on some spectacular bullfights.

Kurt Tucholsky

Italy has managed to create a society that combines a number of the least appealing aspects of socialism with practically all of the vices of capitalism.

Gore Vidal

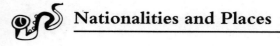 **Nationalities and Places**

Apparently, one in five people in the world is Chinese and there are five people in my family, so it must be one of them. It's either my mum or dad or my older brother Colin or my younger brother Ho-Cha-Chu. But I think it's Colin.

Tommy Cooper

A Canadian is a man who leaves culture to his wife.

Brendan Behan

We English are good at forgiving our enemies; it releases us from the obligation of liking our friends.

P. D. James

The way I understand it, the Russians are sort of a combination of evil and incompetence – like the Post Office with tanks.

Emo Philips

Philadelphia should be abandoned.

Frank Lloyd Wright

The motto of England should be 'Above all no enthusiasm.'

Constant Lambert

Speech therapy in the United States is merely preparation for a future career as a homosexual.

David Sedaris

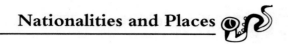

Thinking is the most unhealthy thing in the world and people die of it just as they die of any other disease Fortunately, in England at any rate, thought is not catching.

Oscar Wilde

You must look out in Britain that you are not cheated by the charioteers.

Cicero

Her Russian husband denied drinking seven bottles of vodka at a sitting, but that six was a different matter.

Giles Whittel

My pub, the Douglas Arms in Bethesda, Gwynedd, still accepts old money. When decimalisation came in in 1971, I decided not to join.

Geoffrey Davies

A slogan is a good old American substitute for the facts.

Jacob Braude

The Royal Family – it gives you something to ignore, doesn't it?

Eric W. Baker

Scotsmen are sour, stingy, depressing beggars who parade around in schoolgirls' skirts with nothing on underneath.

P. J. O'Rourke

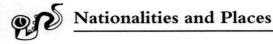

Nationalities and Places

Women wrestlers are the only real attempt at culture on American television.

Robert Morley

The Albanians love Norman Wisdom but funnily enough the Romanians hate him. In 1968 there was a war between Romania and Albania called the Grimsdale War.

Paul Merton

The United States has never lost a war in which mules were used.

P. J. O'Rourke

I cannot understand why I flunked American history. When I was young there was so little of it.

George Burns

In Paris they have chairs and tables out in the street. In Liverpool we call that eviction.

Ken Dodd

I must have Irish blood in me. Every time I speak in public I end up sounding like James Joyce.

George W. Bush

It took me five years to learn to spell Chattanooga. Then we moved to Albuquerque.

Joe Morrison

It's over, and can't be helped, and that's one consolation, as they always say in Turkey, when they cut the wrong man's head off.

Charles Dickens

The Brazilians aren't as good as they used to be, or as they are now.

Kenny Dalglish

I'll bet what motivated the British to colonise so much of the world is that they were just looking for a decent meal.

Martha Harrison

The difference between toast and Italians is that you can make soldiers out of toast.

Peter Ball

I was standing beside this fellow in a bar in Belfast and I said to him, 'You're not from round here, are you?' 'No,' he replied, 'but how on earth did you know that?' 'You just left your drink down,' I said to him.

Frank Carson

When Abraham Lincoln was murdered, the assassin shouted in Latin as he leapt on the stage. This convinced me that there was still hope for America.

Matthew Arnold

The so-called philosophy of India has found its natural home in Los Angeles, the capital of American idiots.

H. L. Mencken

Nationalities and Places

The cold of the polar regions was nothing to the chill of an English bedroom.

Fridtjof Nansen

Australia must be so pretty with all the dear little kangaroos flying about. Agatha has just found it on the map. What a curious shape it is? Just like the packing case.

Oscar Wilde

Living in Manchester is a totally incomprehensible choice for any free human being to make.

Melford Stevenson

McFee, whose chief delusion is that Edinburgh is the Athens of the North, took offence at my description of Edinburgh as the Reykjavik of the South.

Tom Stoppard

The Alps are objects of appallingly bad taste.

Oscar Wilde

I'm not saying our council house is far from the city, but our rent man is a Norwegian.

Les Dawson

In Bradford, they have to wait for snow before they can take a census.

Bernard Manning

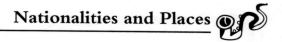

My favourite contestant in the Miss World competition was the parabolic Miss Venezuela.

David Newby

Southport is like Blackpool with O-levels. I won't say it's rough but last night there I got mugged by a nun.

Les Dawson

The Army has carried the American ideal to its logical conclusion. Not only do they prohibit discrimination on grounds of race, creed and colour, but also on ability.

Tom Lehrer

A Red Indian always sleeps with his head towards the fire to keep his wig warm.

Groucho Marx

Hooliganism is not a British disease – we simply perfected it.

Laurie Graham

I would love to speak Italian but I can't. So I just grew some underarm hair instead.

Sue Kolinsky

A blaspheming Frenchman is a spectacle more pleasing to the Lord than a praying Englishman.

Heinrich Heine

Like all New York hotel lady cashiers she had red hair and had been disappointed in her first husband.

Al Capp

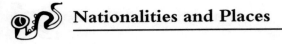

Nationalities and Places

Last week in Russia we saw our names spelt in the Acrylic alphabet. Quite a sight.

Alistair Alexander

Deprived of my British citizenship, I rang up the Irish Embassy and asked if I could have Irish citizenship. 'Bejasus, yes' an official replied, 'we're terrible short of people.'

Spike Milligan

A German singer! I should as soon expect to get pleasure from the neighing of my horse.

Frederick the Great

In Scotland, Spring can fade imperceptibly into Autumn.

Richard Baker

New York is my Lourdes, where I go for spiritual refreshment – a place where you're not likely to be bitten by a wild goat.

Brendan Behan

The mail in Ireland used to be handled by hand, but now it's handled manually.

John Hines

Drunken Russians climbing in and out at every station; enormous ladies being hoisted up onto the upper bunks and falling back on top of everyone; the smell of the feet, the state of the lavatories and above all the incessant singing of the peasants.

Robert Morley

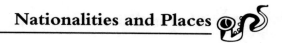

The Atlantic Ocean was disappointing.

Oscar Wilde

The barbarians who broke up the Roman Empire did not arrive a day too soon.

Ralph Waldo Emerson

France is a relatively small and eternally quarrelsome country in Western Europe, fountainhead of rationalist political manias, militarily impotent, historically inglorious, democratically bankrupt, and Communist-infiltrated from top to bottom.

William F. Buckley

The only interesting thing that can happen in a Swiss bedroom is suffocation by feather mattress.

Dalton Trumbo

Niagara is pure Walt.

Robert Morley

The English sent all their bores abroad, and acquired the Empire as punishment.

Edward Bond

Venice would be a fine city if only it were drained.

Ulysses S. Grant

Nationalities and Places

I have lived in poverty for 20 years in the illiterate and malignant wilderness that is called Dublin whose inhabitants care nothing for the things of the spirit. They blathered about poetry but they knew as much about it as my arse knows about snipe shooting.

Patrick Kavanagh

In Darlington the shops seemed to be full of nothing but postcards of a great train crash that had occurred there.

Robert Morley

There is no chance of an English girl winning Miss World. The meal I had in my hotel was digusting. I was sick afterwards. Their food isn't fit for hamsters.

Silvio Maric

I can confirm that Russell Crowe does not wear deodorant. In Australia I believe they call it animal magnetism.

Joan Rivers

We travel writers are required, by law, to describe Hong Kong harbour as teeming.

Dave Barry

The authorities in New York City ought to pair up all the street people who mumble to themselves so they'd look like they were having conversations.

Lily Tomlin

Among the countless blessings I thank God for, my failure to find a house in Ireland comes first.

Evelyn Waugh

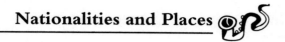

One always expects that just around the next corner there would be something fascinating to look at, and of course there never is; this is the whole charm of Australia. And Sydney – you might as well call a city Bert.

Robert Morley

The trouble with England is that it leads the world in nothing but decline.

Martin Amis

The Welsh remain the only race whom you can vilify without being called a racist.

A.N. Wilson

Politics

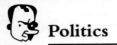

Politics

The punishment for those who are too smart to engage in politics is to be governed by those who are dumber.

Plato

We women politicians have got the men out there worrying that we'll all have PMS on the same day and blow up the town.

Barbara Carr

The Marxist law of distribution of wealth is that shortages will be divided equally among the peasants.

John Guftason

Joseph Chamberlain was dangerous as an enemy, untrustworthy as a friend, but fatal as a colleague.

Hercules Robinson

Joseph McCarthy is the only major politician in the country who can be labeled 'liar' without fear of libel.

Joseph Alsop

How can I vote Liberal? I just hold my nose and mark the ballot paper.

Frank Underhill

Mr Chamberlain loves the working man; he loves to see him work.

Winston Churchill

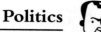

We hang petty thieves and appoint the great ones to public office.

Aesop

Italian communists are slightly to the right of English Liberals.

John Mortimer

Half of those who attended De Valera's funeral came to confirm that he dead. The other half came to ensure that he was buried.

Barry Desmond

The House of Lords is a refuge for cattle robbers, land thieves and court prostitutes.

Jack Jones

Russian democracy is vastly superior to American democracy. In Russia we know the result of the elections a week before they take place. In America they don't know the result of the election a week after it takes place.

Vladimir Putin

Margaret Thatcher should be hung up by the bollocks.

Jo Brand

There is only one party in this coalition.

Henry McLeish

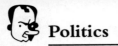

If you open that Pandora's box you never know what Trojan horses will jump out.

Ernest Bevin

It was not a lie. I was merely being economical with the truth.

Robert Armstrong

Welcome to President Bush, Mrs Bush and my fellow astronauts.

Dan Quayle

Most Conservatives believe that a creche is something that happens between two Range Rovers in Tunbridge Wells.

Caroline Shorten

If Gandhi were alive today he would approve of the SDP.

Richard Attenborough

When the Berlin Wall fell and Germany was reunited, the Stasi, the former East German secret police, made wonderful taxi-drivers. All you had to do was tell them your name and they immediately knew where you lived.

Paul Merton

I apologise for the intelligence of my remarks, Sir Thomas. I had forgotten that you are a Member of Parliament.

George Sanders

A chill ran along the Labour back benches looking for a spine to run up.

Winnie Ewing

The ship follows Soviet custom: it is riddled with class distinctions so subtle it takes a trained Marxist to appreciate them.

Paul Theroux

Edward the Eighth was far to the right of my husband.

Diana Mosley

I am always on the job.

Margaret Thatcher

What this country needs is more unemployed politicians.

Angela Davis

These are trying moments, and it seems to me a defect in our much-famed constitution to have to part with an admirable government like Lord Salisbury's for no question of any importance, or any particular reason, merely on account of the number of votes.

Queen Victoria

The election isn't very far off when a candidate can recognise you across the street.

Kin Hubbard

Mrs Thatcher can be compared with Florence Nightingale. She walks through the hospitals as a lady with a lamp – unfortunately, in her case it is a blowlamp.

Denis Healey

Where Caligula made his horse a consul, Long's constituents have made the posterior of a horse a US senator.

Senator Glass

I think the voters misunderestimate me.

George W. Bush

The mystery of government is not how Washington works but how to make it stop.

P. J. O'Rourke

Calvin Coolidge didn't say much, and when he did he didn't say much.

Will Rogers

It doesn't matter if Margaret Thatcher or Michael Heseltine is Tory leader. They are both millionaires and both peroxide blondes.

Dennis Skinner

When I am abroad I always make it a rule never to criticise or attack the government of my country. I make up for lost time when I am at home.

Winston Churchill

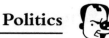

If John Major was drowning, his whole life would pass in front of him and he wouldn't be in it.

Dave Allen

The difference between a New Labour back-bench MP and a supermarket trolley is that a supermarket trolley has a mind of its own.

Peter Lilley

The vice-president is just a spare tyre on the automobile of government.

John Garner

Corruption is the most infallible symptom of constitutional liberty.

Edward Gibbon

Paddy Ashdown is the only party leader to be a trained killer. Although to be fair Mrs Thatcher was self-taught.

Charles Kennedy

You suddenly realise you are no longer in government when you get into the back of your car and it doesn't go anywhere.

Malcolm Rifkind

We've got a carrot and stick policy on Saddam Hussein. And the carrot is, if he pulls out, he doesn't get the stick.

James Baker

Politics

I believe in compulsory cannibalism. If people were forced to eat what they killed, there would be no more wars.

Abbie Hoffman

When John Prescott was only a month old he was left on a doorstep for three days and three nights in a little basket and nobody picked him up; so his father and mother took him in again.

Greg Knight

If you want to succeed in politics, you must keep your conscience under control.

David Lloyd George

When David Mellor loses his seat, he can earn an excellent living delivering gorillagrams without the need for a suit.

Paul Flynn

The honourable member for Bourke, who is believed to have committed every crime in the book, except the one we could so easily have forgiven him – suicide.

Henry Parks

John Collins was a man of great statue.

Thomas Menino

The only thing that Roy Jenkins ever fought for was a table for two at the Mirabelle.

Greg Knight

A politician is an acrobat. He keeps his balance by doing the opposite of what he says.

Maurice Barres

Gordon Brown bases his politics on the Dolly Parton School of Economics – an unbelievable figure, blown out of all proportion, with no visible means of support.

Kenneth Clarke

We've got the kind of President who thinks arms control means some kind of deodorant.

Patricia Schroeder

If John Prescott remains in office much longer, cars will have to be preceded by a man walking in front of them singing the 'Red Flag'.

Keith Waterhouse

Is it not the case that those councillors found guilty of fraud are the only people left in the Labour Party with genuine convictions?

William Hague

The Government, in due course, acted promptly.

Geoffrey Giles

The Natural Law Party claims to have achieved the art of levitation, but critics have described this as suspiciously close to jumping up and down.

Peter Davis

The Natural Law Party is best known for transcendental meditation and failure at the polls.

John Burns

I recognise and acknowledge Eton's talent for getting stupid boys into Parliament.

Auberon Waugh

The politician who steals is worse than a thief. He is a fool. With the grand opportunities all around for a man with political pull there's no excuse for stealin' a cent.

George Plunkitt

For those of you who don't know what the Ku Klux Klan is – that's people who get outta bed in the middle of the night and take the sheet with them. You always see pictures of them wearing pointed hoods? Those hoods are flat! It's the heads that are pointed.

Dick Gregory

There ought to be one day, just one, when there is open season on senators.

Will Rogers

Politics is the art of staying out of jail.

Can Yucel

Liberals will defend to the death your right to agree with them.

Ronald Reagan

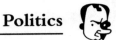

A life peer is like a mule with neither pride of ancestry nor hope of posterity.

Lord Shackleton

Say what you have to say and the first time you come to a sentence with a grammatical ending – sit down.

Winston Churchill

Damn your principles! Stick to your party.

Benjamin Disraeli

Creative semantics is the key to contemporary government; it consists of talking in strange tongues lest the public learn the inevitable inconveniently early.

George Will

The President is going to lead us out of this recovery.

Dan Quayle

In the US everyone is considered innocent until appointed to a public position by the President.

William Crowe

I always knew Lloyd George had won the war, but until I read his memoirs, I did not know that he had won it single-handed.

Margot Asquith

For the MP who claims to have a 'orrible 'eadache, I would prescribe a couple of aspirates.

F. H. Smith

Politics

The Presidency is the greased pig in the field game of American politics.

Ambrose Bierce

Women politicians remind one of the British tramp steamers decorated for the Queen's birthday.

H. L. Mencken

A bill to make attendance at the House of Commons compulsory for MPs has just been passed by three votes to two.

Anthony Jay

A stateswoman is a woman who meddles in public affairs.

Samuel Johnson

Denis Howell could easily be mistaken for the traditional plumber with a cleft palate who has lost his dentures down the lavatory.

Auberon Waugh

I can't be bought, but I can be rented.

Don O 'Shaughnessy

The punishment in Massachusetts for reckless driving appears to be re-election to the Senate.

Emo Philips

The cure for admiring the House of Lords is to go and look at it.

Walter Bagehot

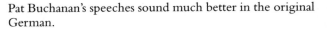

Pat Buchanan's speeches sound much better in the original German.

Molly Ivers

We may not be able to imagine how our lives could be more frustrating or complex – but Congress can.

Cullen Hightower

The best argument against democracy is a five minute talk with the average voter.

Winston Churchill

Did you sleep with Bill Clinton? No. Neither did I. Small world, isn't it?

Rita Rudner

Left-wingers are incapable of conspiring because they are all egomaniacs.

Norman Mailer

Democracy used to be a good thing, but now it has gotten into the wrong hands.

Jesse Helms

The vice-presidency is like the last cookie on the plate. Everybody insists he won't take it, but somebody always does.

Bill Vaughan

I used to be the next President of the United States.

Al Gore

Just be thankful you're not getting all the government you 're paying for.

Will Rogers

I've decided to take up a life of crime, but I can't decide on which political party to join.

Roy Brown

The biggest mistake that Bill Clinton made was not getting Teddy Kennedy to drive Monica Lewinsky home.

Denis Leary

A senator is a person who makes laws in Washington when not doing time.

Mark Twain

Who is to blame for the killings? The killers are to blame.

Dan Quayle

I make more money than the Prime Minister but then I give a lot more pleasure than he does.

W. S. Gilbert

Man is the only animal that laughs and has a state legislature.

Samuel Butler

Democracy means that anyone can grow up to be president and anyone who doesn't grow up can be vice-president.

Johnny Carson

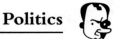

The KGB have just arrested the fellow who broke a bottle of ketchup over Gorbachev 's head.

Alexei Sayle

For every action there is an equal and opposite government program.

Bob Wells

I don't make predictions. I never have and I never will.

Tony Blair

Has Monica Lewinsky blown it for the President?

Scott Chisholm

Lord Dartmouth stayed in the cabinet long enough only to prostitute his character and authenticate his hypocrisy.

Horace Walpole

I intend to open Brazil up to democracy, and anyone who is against this I will jail, I will crush.

Joao Figueredo

J. Edgar Hoover should be trusted as much as a rattlesnake with a silencer on his rattle.

Dean Acheson

A woman has narrowly failed to assassinate President Gerald Ford. There are too many guns in this country in the hands of people who don't know how to use them.

Hubert Humphrey

You don't have to attend meetings of the Labour Party, just give them your VISA number.

Ken Loach

A Japanese children's TV show features a piece of talking excrement that keeps popping up from the toilet to express strange platitudes only an adult can fathom. You're thinking 'Hey! Sounds like Henry Kissinger.'

Dave Barry

Bill Clinton is going round with a pair of ladies' panties on his arm. It's the patch, he's trying to quit.

Sam Donaldson

I'm back in politics and you knew I was coming. On my way here I passed a sign: THE MUMMY RETURNS.

Margaret Thatcher

Congresspersons would cheerfully vote to spend millions to develop a working artificial haemorrhoid, as long as the money would be spent in their districts.

Dave Barry

Religion

Religion

Evelyn Waugh was the nastiest-tempered man in England, Catholic or Protestant.

James Lees-Milne

He could never make up his mind between suicide and an equally drastic course of action known as Father D'Arcy.

Muriel Spark

My ambition is to rescue God from religion.

Sinead O'Connor

Moss Hart's country garden looks like what God would have done if He'd had the money.

Alexander Woollcott

I am told that printers' readers no longer exist because clergymen are no longer unfrocked for sodomy.

Evelyn Waugh

There may have been disillusionments in the lives of the mediaeval saints, but they would scarcely have been better pleased if they could have foreseen that their names would be associated nowadays chiefly with racehorses and the cheaper clarets.

Saki

I definitely want Brooklyn christened, but I don't know into what religion yet.

David Beckham

Religion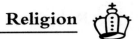

My father was not at all devout. But he saw Jesus as quite a good chap, as the honorable member for Galilee South.

Malcolm Muggeridge

What would happen if Moses were alive today? He'd go up Mount Sinai, come back with the Ten Commandments, and spend the next eight years trying to get published.

Robert Orben

The prison warder asked me my religion and I replied 'agnostic'. He remarked with a sigh: 'Well, there are many religions, but I suppose we all worship the same God.'

Bertrand Russell

I want to play the role of Jesus. I'm a logical choice. I look the part. I'm a Jew and I'm a comedian. And I'm an atheist, so I'd be able to look at the character objectively.

Charlie Chaplin

I love gentiles. In fact, one of my favourite activities is Protestant spotting.

Mel Brooks

What some preachers lack in depth they make up for in length.

Mark Twain

As far as religion is concerned, I'm a Baptist and a good friend of the Pope, and I always wear a Jewish star for luck.

Louis Armstrong

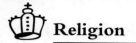

I do not fast during Lent because although I have a Catholic soul, I have a Lutheran stomach.

Desiderius Erasmus

God created Eve because when He had finished creating Adam, He stepped back, scratched His head and said, 'I think I can do better than that.'

Phyllis Diller

We need a new cosmology. New Gods. New Sacraments. Another drink.

Patti Smith

If God wanted me to touch my toes, he would have put them on my knees.

Roseanne Barr

They say altar wine contains Glauber's salts so as priests won't get the taste and break their pledges.

Dominic Behan

What a hell of a heaven it will be, when they get all those hypocrites assembled there.

Mark Twain

When Frank Sinatra goes to heaven, he's going to give God a hard time for making him bald.

Marlon Brando

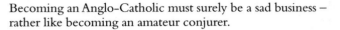

Becoming an Anglo-Catholic must surely be a sad business – rather like becoming an amateur conjurer.

John Strachey

Is there an afterlife? Well there's an afterbirth, so why shouldn't there be an afterlife?

Kevin MacAleer

After his long fast, the toad has a very spiritual look, like a strict Anglo-Catholic towards the end of Lent.

George Orwell

I would have more respect for the Pope if he wore a white cotton teeshirt emblazoned in red with the legend: INFALLIBLE BUT NOT INFLEXIBLE.

Fran Lebowitz

God never shut one door but He closed another.

James Plunkett

To steal from the rich is a sacred and religious act.

Jerry Rubin

I am an unbeliever but I sometimes have doubts.

George Bernard Shaw

♔ Religion

Ever since he was a child, Paddy had wanted to be a priest, but he was refused entry into Maynooth seminary because of his height. He wasn't able to reach the altar. Anyway he could never stand all that early morning drinking.

James McKeon

Both Testaments are full of pundits, prophets, disciples, favourite sons, Solomons, Isaiahs, Davids, Pauls – but my God, who besides Jesus really knew which end was up? Nobody.

J. D. Salinger

A feast is a religious celebration usually signalised by gluttony and drunkenness, frequently in honour of some holy person distinguished for abstemiousness.

Ambrose Bierce

The devil is the father of lies, but he neglected to patent the idea and now the business suffers from severe competition, mostly from politicians.

Josh Billings

A definition of Hell is a garage motor mechanic with greasy hands and no steering wheel to wipe them on.

Jimmy Elliot

The wages of sin are death, but by the time taxes are taken out, all you are left with is just a sort of tired feeling.

Paula Poundstone

Religion

I don't know as much as God, but I know as much as God knew at my age.

Milton Shulman

A lot of pillars of the Church end up as two columns in the *Evening Standard*.

William Inge

And on the eighth day God said: 'OK Murphy, you can take over now.'

Michael Redmond

Repent! If you have already repented please disregard this notice.

George Carlin

And God said, 'Let there be vodka' and there was vodka and He saw that it was good. Then God said 'Let there be light' and He said 'Whoa, too much light.'

Robin Williams

Why assume so glibly that the God who presumably created the Universe is still running it – He may have finished it and then turned it over to lesser gods to operate. Many human institutions are turned over to grossly inferior men – for example most universities and newspapers.

H. L. Mencken

My church accepts all denominations – fivers, tenners, twenties.

Dave Allen

Religion

Sunday School is a prison in which children do penance for the evil conscience of their parents.

H. L. Mencken

I broke up with my boyfriend for religious reasons – he thought he was God and I didn't.

Rita Rudner

Each of his sermons was better than the next.

James Montgomery

My wife and I are two well-behaved God-fearing people who always keep the Ten Commandments – five each.

Mitch Murray

An atheist is a man who has no invisible means of support.

John Buchan

Meeting Orson Welles is like meeting God without dying.

Dorothy Parker

Lord, grant me the courage and tenacity of a weed.

Karel Capek

God gave man the gift of Sloth in exchange for his rib.

Robert Morley

My favourite characters in the Bible are King David, Delilah, and Charlton Heston.

George Burns

Religion

Unitarianism is, in effect, the worst of one kind of atheism joined to the worst of one kind of Calvinism, like two asses tied tail to tail.

Samuel Taylor Coleridge

Happiness is having a legitimate excuse for not attending a Bar Mitzvah.

George Burns

Science and Technology

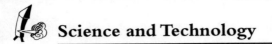

Science and Technology

Birthdays are good for you. Statistics show that people who have the most birthdays live longest.

John Paulos

The genitals themselves have not undergone the development of the rest of the human form in the direction of beauty.

Sigmund Freud

Neil Armstrong was the first man to walk on the moon. I was the first man to piss his pants on the moon.

Buzz Aldrin

When decorating I always use a step-ladder. I don't really get on with my real ladder.

Harry Hill

Artificial Intelligence is the study of how to make real computers act like the ones in the movies.

David Arnold

Autumn wasps are the most dangerous, delirious and resentful that all the children have gone back to school.

Dylan Moran

If it looks like an elephant, sounds like an elephant, and there's half a ton of steaming manure on the floor, it's probably an elephant.

A. A. Gill

Science and Technology

The terrorist who mailed a letter bomb with insufficient postage wins a Darwin Award when he opens the returned package.

Wendy Northcutt

You know when you step on a mat in the supermarket and the door opens? For years, I thought it was a coincidence.

Richard Jeni

I think the aardvark just made up that name when he heard that Noah was taking the animals onto the Ark in alphabetical order.

Matt King

The marvels of modern technology include the development of a soda can which, when discarded, will last forever, and a $7000 car which, when properly cared for, will rust out in two or three years.

Paul Harwitz

The human brain is merely a device to prevent the ears grating on one another.

Peter DeVries

The only thing that continues to give us more for our money is the weighing machine.

George Clark

In relation to computers I am firmly of the opinion that Macintosh is Catholic and that MS-DOS is Protestant.

Umberto Eco

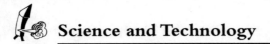

The first pull on the cord always sends the curtains in the wrong direction.

Andrew Boyle

Pilot Rule No. 1: Always try to keep the number of landings you make equal to the number of takeoffs you've made.

Paul Andrews

Is my latest child a boy or a girl? Yes.

Bertrand Russell

At the moment it's just a Notion, but with a bit of backing I think I could turn it into a Concept, and then an Idea.

Woody Allen

Edison's first major invention in 1877 was the phonograph, which could be found in thousands of American homes, where it basically sat until 1923, when the record was invented.

Dave Barry

Ask my wife to postpone dying for just a few minutes – I am nearly finished proving this theorem.

Carl Friedrich Gauss

Concerned parents should demand the removal of arsenic from the periodic table of the elements. Our schoolchildren, some as young as the fourth grade, are being exposed to this deadly element in their science classes.

Aileen Nilsen

Science and Technology

Thirty-six per cent of the American public believes that boiling radioactive milk makes it safe to drink.

Jon Miller

Basically, a tool is an object that enables you to take advantage of the laws of physics and mechanics in such a way that you can seriously injure yourself.

Dave Barry

They say the Universe started with a big bang. I hope everybody stood well back.

Eddie Izzard

If scientists can put a man on the moon, why can't they figure out which kid hit the other first?

Bruce Lansky

Astronomy teaches us the correct use of the sun and the planets.

Stephen Leacock

Goldfish always die. Don't even bother to decant them from the plastic bag.

Jenny Eclair

Logic is the art of going wrong with confidence.

Morris Kline

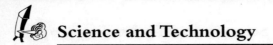

Today's robots are very primitive, capable of understanding only a few simple instructions like 'go left', 'go right', and 'build car'.

John Sladek

I'd rather have a goddam horse than a car. A horse is at least human, for God's sake.

J. D. Salinger

Nuclear fission is like kissing your wife. Nuclear fusion is like kissing your mistress.

Robert B. Macauley

A body on vacation tends to remain on vacation unless acted upon by an outside force.

Carol Reichel

The sun got confused about daylight saving time. It rose twice. Everything had two shadows.

Steven Wright

Resistance is useless if less than 1 ohm.

Richard Feynman

Einstein's Law supercedes Newton's Law; Murphy's Law supercedes Einstein's Law.

Arthur Carroll

It is impossible to travel faster than light, and certainly not desirable as one's hat would keep blowing off.

Woody Allen

Electricity is actually made up of extremely tiny particles, called electrons, which you cannot see with the naked eye unless you've been drinking.

Dave Barry

Pilot Rule No 2: In the ongoing battle between objects made of aluminium travelling at hundreds of miles per hour and the ground going at zero miles per hour, the ground has yet to lose.

Paul Andrews

The Internet is a great way of getting on the net.

Bob Dole

A virus is only doing its job.

David Cronenberg

The computer can do more work faster than a human being because it doesn't have to answer the phone.

Joey Adams

Statistics is the mathematical theory of ignorance.

Morris Kline

Legend has it that the atom was split when a bunch of scientists working late decided to order pizza.

Fran Lebowitz

Women read instruction books, and this is the single biggest difference between the sexes.

Jeremy Clarkson

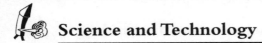

The only way a mathematician can get publicity is by shooting somebody.

Thomas Nicely

People who spend most of their natural lives riding iron bicycles get their personalities mixed up with the personalities of their bicycles as a result of the interchanging of the mollycules of each of them.

Flann O'Brien

Shelley and Keats were the last English poets who were at all up to date in their chemical knowledge.

J. B. S. Haldane

God exists since mathematics is consistent, but the Devil exists since we cannot prove that mathematics is consistent.

André Weil

What happens when a big asteroid hits Earth? Judging from realistic simulations involving a sledge hammer and a common laboratory frog, we can assume it will be pretty bad.

Dave Barry

Computers are like humans – they do everything except think.

John Von Neumann

It is too bad that we cannot cut the patient in half in order to compare two regimens of treatment.

Bela Schick

Science and Technology

Let us stop bequeathing our brains to science; science has enough trouble with the brains they already have.

Walt Kelly

Computers of the future will weigh no more than 1.5 tons.

J. D. Percival

Automatic simply means you cannot repair it yourself.

Frank Capra

My garage's motto seems to be 'If it ain't broke, we'll break it.'

Jerry Seinfeld

The universe has fascinated mankind for many, many years, dating back to the very earliest episodes of *Star Trek*.

Dave Barry

I have found the missing link between animal and civilised man. It is us.

Konrad Lorenz

It has been claimed that a million monkeys banging on a million typewriters will eventually reproduce the entire works of Shakespeare. Now, thanks to the Internet, we know this is not true.

Robert Wilensky

The hazards of computing are limited only by your imagination.

Pete Martin

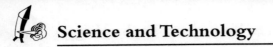

They asked me in the physics examination what the Uncertainty Principle was. I answered that I wasn't quite sure.

Simon Davidson

'Cellophane wrapped' means you've got to tear it open with your teeth.

Leonard Levinson

It's only when you look at an ant through a magnifying glass on a sunny day that you realise how often they burst into flames.

Harry Hill

As the zero said to the eight, 'nice belt man'.

Peter Cashman

If you lock a hundred monkeys in a room with a hundred typewriters, after a week you'll have a hundred dead monkeys.

Brian Twomey

I've got a problem. I've got an endangered animal that eats only endangered plants.

Steven Wright

The chief function of the body is to carry the brain around.

Thomas Edison

Four thirds of all people don't understand fractions.

Steven Wright

A duck's quack doesn't echo, and nobody knows why.

Ed Bluestone

If you go back in time, be careful not to step in anything.

Matt Groening

I hear they can now make motor fuel from horse manure. I don't know how efficient it is but it's sure as hell going to put a stop to siphoning.

Billie Holiday

Those fax machines are dangerous. I got my tie caught in one the other day and three minutes later I found myself in Hong Kong.

Ken Dodd

All men can fly, but sadly only in one direction – down.

Sydney Harris

Here's to the higher mathematics – may it never be of any use to anyone.

Duff Cooper

Imagine if birds were tickled by feathers. You'd see a whole flock of birds come by laughing hysterically.

Steven Wright

There's something funny going on out there – when did you ever see a young pigeon?

Tom Lehrer

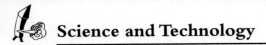

The average human being has one breast and one testicle.

Robert Murphy

I'm glad cavepeople didn't invent TV, because they would have just sat around and watched talk shows all day instead of inventing tools.

Dave James

There's a new Bill Clinton computer on the market. It has a six inch hard drive but no memory.

David Letterman

Albert Einstein was my pupil. He had no aptitude for long division. How he talked his way into a Nobel Prize is beyond me, but then it's like the man says, 'It's what you know...'

Karl Arbeiter

Everything in space is weightless but would a really fat astronaut just weigh a little bit?

Patrick Murray

The Bureau of Incomplete Statistics reports that one out of three.

Aidan Moran

Physics is like sex; sure it may give some practical results, but that's not why you do it.

Richard Feynman

Science and Technology

I'm worried that the Universe will soon need replacing. It's not holding a charge.

Edward Chilton

All power corrupts, but we need electricity.

Haythum Khalid

If the universe is expanding, why can't I find a parking space?

Woody Allen

As far as we know, no computer has ever had an undetected error.

Bill Murphy

I never met a robot I didn't like.

Isaac Asimov

How can you tell you've run out of invisible ink?

Steven Wright

Microsoft is the biggest virus ever created by man.

Bud Minton

For NASA, space is still a high priority.

Dan Quayle

I thought RAM DISK was an installation procedure.

Dave Barry

Is fuel efficiency what we need most desperately? I say what we need is a car that can be shot when it breaks down.

Russell Baker

I don't know a lot about genetics, but not calling when you're supposed to is a trait definitely attached to the Y chromosome.

Cynthia Heimel

Get yourself a DNA testing kit so that when your man comes home at night you can do a little testing on his underwear to see where he has been.

Diane Conway

This year I'm a star; what will I be next year? A black hole?

Woody Allen

The goal of all inanimate objects is to resist man and ultimately to defeat him.

Russell Baker

Statistics is the most exact of the false sciences.

Jean Cau

Nuclear-powered vacuum cleaners will probably be a reality within ten years.

Alex Lewyt

A nuclear power plant is infinitely safer than eating, because 33 people choke to death on food every year.

Dixy Lee Roy

Science and Technology

The first Zambian astronaut will be on the Moon by 1965 using my own catapult-based firing system. They will be acclimatised to space travel in a 40-gallon oil drum rolling down a hill. I also make them swing from the end of a long rope – at its highest point, I cut the rope, producing the sensation of a free fall.

Edward Nkoloso

Everything that goes up must come down. But there comes a time when not everything that's down can come up.

George Burns

I believe that lobsters are the result of a terrible genetic accident involving nuclear radiation and cockroaches.

Dave Barry

It takes millions of sperm to fertilise an egg because not one of them will stop to ask for directions.

Rita Rudner

The sun is still there even at night – it's just that we can't see it.

Mike Lepine

Red sky at night, arsonists at the B&Q warehouse.

Mark Leigh

Social Behaviour and Manners

Social Behaviour...

For the last twenty years Elsie de Wolfe's age has been legendary.

Janet Flanner

Henry Ward Beecher is a remarkably handsome man when he is in the full tide of sermonising, and his face is lit up with animation, but he is as homely as a singed cat when he isn't doing anything.

Mark Twain

I could have wept, parting with him, but I could not get at my handkerchief without unbuttoning my boatcloak and that was inconvenient.

Jane Carlyle

Within minutes, several eyewitnesses were on the scene.

Adam Boulton

Bores can be divided into two classes; those who have their own particular subject, and those who do not need a subject.

A.A. Milne

If you want to be a leader with a large following, just obey the speed limit on a winding, two-lane road.

Charles Farr

You'd be hoarse listening to her.

Maureen Potter

There is nothing more dangerous than a resourceful idiot.

Scott Adams

During a communal crisis, keep looking shocked and move slowly towards the cakes.

Homer Simpson

I don't get angry and I don't hate people. If something bad happens, I forget it right away. Or at least ten minutes later.

George Burns

The most important thing when you are going to do something brave is to have someone on hand to witness it.

Michael Howard

Never trust a man who combs his hair from his left armpit.

Theodore Roosevelt

He was the sort of man that Spooner would have referred to as a shining wit.

Hugh Leonard

He's such a perfect host. He always makes his guests feel at home, even when he wishes they were.

Richard Briers

The quotation of two or three lines of a stanza from Spenser's *Faerie Queene* is probably as good an all-round silencer as anything.

Stephen Potter

If you do your job right, only two people show up at your funeral.

Lewis Lapham

Social Behaviour...

I managed capitally at dinner but I had a knife and two forks left at the end.

William Ridge

Gentlemen, Ravanelli may look like an idiot, he may behave like an idiot, but don't let that fool you; he really is an idiot.

Groucho Marx

To ensure peace of mind, ignore the rules and regulations.

George Ade

Weddings are sadder than funerals because they remind you of your own wedding. You can't be reminded of your own funeral because it hasn't happened. But weddings always make me cry.

Brendan Behan

In the tenth century, the Grand Vizier of Persia took his entire library with him wherever he went. The 117,000-volume library was carried by camels trained to walk in alphabetical order.

Geoff Tibbals

The sweetest words in the English language are: I told you so.

Gore Vidal

Knowledge is power if you know it about the right person.

Ethel Mumford

You could tell the sort of club it was. The bouncers were outside throwing the drunks in.

Les Dawson

For 'You really must come and see us soon' read 'If you call us we'll pretend we're out'.

Stephen Burgen

No man goes before his time – unless the boss leaves early.

Groucho Marx

Duty is what one expects of others, it is not what one does oneself.

Oscar Wilde

It's not nice to joke about fat people – but they can't catch you.

Marsha Warfield

I'm a controversial figure. My friends either dislike me or hate me.

Oscar Levant

Give him an evasive answer. Tell him to go **** himself.

W. C. Fields

Come again when you can't stay so long.

Walter Sickert

The experience of Lord Snowdon will be a lesson to all of us men to be careful not to marry ladies in very high position.

Idi Amin

Yes, I admit my mother was a cook, but I assure you that she was a very bad cook.

Louis Thiers

While queueing in our supermarket for fresh peas, I was appalled to see the lady in front of me individually selecting the best pods. Surely one should take a random selection, so leaving a decent choice for other shoppers?

M. G. Edwards

Some people pay a compliment as if they expected a receipt.

Kin Hubbard

I hate people who point at their wrist while asking for the time. I know where my watch is, buddy, where is yours? Do I point at my crotch when I ask where the can is?

Denis Leary

One of the most shameful utterances to stem from the human mouth is Will Rogers's 'I never met a man I didn't like.'

S. J. Perelman

My father spent the last twenty years of his life writing letters. If someone thanked him for a present, he thanked them for thanking him and there was no end to the exchange but death.

Evelyn Waugh

I was sad because I had no shoes, until I met a man who had no feet. So I said, 'Got any shoes you're not using?'

Steven Wright

A friend in need is an acquaintance.

Mariella Frostrup

It is impossible to disagree with someone about the ethics of non-violence without wanting to kick his face in.

Christopher Hampton

The other day in the Underground I enjoyed the pleasure of offering my seat to three ladies.

G. K. Chesterton

I know you've heard so much about me, but you can't prove a thing.

Mae West

I've just spent an hour talking to Tallulah Bankhead for a few minutes.

Fred Keating

I like to wear my sideburns behind my ears.

Steven Wright

I am one of those unfortunates to whom death is less hideous than explanation.

Wyndham Lewis

Why doesn't a fellow who says, 'I'm no speechmaker', let it go at that instead of giving a demonstration?

> Kin Hubbard

I threw my cook out of the open window on to the flowerbed below. Good God, I forgot the violets!

> Walter Savage Landor

Joan Crawford always cries a lot. Her tear ducts must be very close to her bladder.

> Bette Davis

The only way to entertain some folk is to listen to them.

> Kin Hubbard

To really annoy people, shout random numbers when somebody is counting something.

> Mike McQueen

Nothing is more irritating than not being invited to a party you wouldn't be seen dead at.

> Bill Vaughan

I declare this thing open – whatever it is.

> Philip Mountbatten

I never take a gift of diamonds from a perfect stranger, but who's perfect?

> Zsa Zsa Gabor

He was phony – everything about him was phony. Even his hair, which looked false, was real.

Brendan Behan

'The Management Would Like to Apologise For Any Inconvenience' suggests that they would like to but are damned if they will.

Stephen Burgen

To know Barbra Streisand is not necessarily to love her.

Rex Reed

I should never be allowed to go out in private.

Randolph Churchill

The life and soul, the man who will never go home while there is one man, woman or glass of anything not yet drunk.

Katherine Whitehorn

It is the solemn duty of every landlord to maintain an adequate supply of roaches. The minimum acceptable roach to tenant ratio is 4,000 to one.

Fran Lebowitz

If a beggar in the street asks you for money, ask him if he has the change of a tenner. When he reaches into his pocket, he is rumbled.

Peter McCormack

Work is a refuge for people with nothing to do.

Oscar Wilde

Social Behaviour...

Always speak your mind – even if you don't mean it.

Mark Twain

Hatred is by far the longest pleasure.

Byron

I prefer to forget both pairs of glasses, and pass my declining years saluting strange women and grandfather clocks.

Ogden Nash

No one really minds seeing a friend fall off the roof.

Mark Twain

You may not be one but you certainly look like one – which is even worse.

Lord Queensberry

Certainly, I enjoyed myself at the party. There was nothing else to enjoy.

George Bernard Shaw

It is generally agreed that 'hello' is an appropriate greeting on entering a room, because if you entered a room and said 'goodbye', it would confuse a lot of people.

Dolph Sharp

He has all the virtues I dislike and none of the vices I admire.

Winston Churchill

Social Behaviour...

Etiquette means behaving yourself a little better than is absolutely essential.

Will Cuppy

I appeared on a Nazi death list with some people I wouldn't have been seen dead with.

Rebecca West

I think she must have been very strictly brought up, she's so desperately anxious to do the wrong thing correctly.

Saki

If you have anything important to tell me, for God's sake begin at the end.

Sara Duncan

Punctuality is the art of guessing how late the other person is going to be.

Faye Copeland

Tell me the history of that frock, dear. It's obviously an old favourite. You were wise to remove the curtain rings.

Edna Everage

So I've tried your patience – you must try mine sometime.

Groucho Marx

Social Behaviour...

Gentlemen know that fresh air should be kept in its proper place – out of doors – and that, God having given us indoors and outdoors, we should not attempt to do away with this distinction.

Rose Macaulay

I am informed that Lady Marlborough will be at home on March 26th. So will I.

George Bernard Shaw

If you enter a room and everyone turns to look at you, then you are not well dressed.

Beau Brummel

To make an enemy, do someone a favour.

James McLaughry

Diderot is a great wit and conversationalist, but nature has denied him one great gift – that of dialogue.

Voltaire

At our first meeting, William Wordsworth was very kind to me and let me hear his conversation.

Elizabeth Barrett

Darling Maimie, Thank you a hundred times for the lovely handkerchiefs. I have tied one to each ball and one to my cock and they look very becoming.

Evelyn Waugh

Social Behaviour...

I've seen guys moving slower than Corey Pavin leaving hotel fires.

Jim Murray

I judge how much a man cares for a woman by the space he allots her under a jointly shared umbrella.

Jimmy Cannon

Please watch your language mother, there are soldiers present.

Barbara Ford

She poured a little social sewage into his ears.

George Meredith

There's something about you I like – I wish I could remember what it is.

J. R. Fox

My grandfather, Frank Lloyd Wright, wore nothing but a red sash on his wedding night. Now that was glamour.

Anne Baxter

The only meeting that ever started on time was held up for an hour while things were explained to people who came in late and didn't know what was going on.

Doug Larson

In dinner talk it is perhaps allowable to fling any faggot on the fire rather than let it go out.

J. M. Barrie

Social Behaviour...

John Daly has the worst haircut I've ever seen in my life and I've seen a few bad ones. It looks like he has a divot over each ear.

David Feherty

My wife tells me that our next door neighbour kisses his wife passionately every morning before he leaves for work. I would do the same but I hardly know the woman.

Henny Youngman

People who haven't spoken to each other for years are on speaking terms again today – including the bride and groom.

Dorothy Parker

Nothing compares to the paperweight as a bad gift. Where are these people working that the papers are just blowing right off their desks? What do you need a paperweight for? Where is all the wind coming from?

Jerry Seinfeld

A bore is a fellow talker who can change the topic of conversation to his subject faster than you can change it back to yours.

Laurence J. Peter

A true friend does not stab you in the back, he stabs you in the front.

Oscar Wilde

Never moon a werewolf.

Mike Binder

The concept behind the mobile phone is that you have absolutely nothing to say and you've got to tell somebody right now.

Jerry Seinfeld

Philosophy teaches us to bear with equanimity the misfortunes of our neighbours.

Oscar Wilde

When lovely woman stoops to folly,
The evening can be awfully jolly.

Mary Demetriadis

The reason women don't play football is that eleven of them would never wear the same outfit in public.

Phyllis Diller

Never settle with words what you can accomplish with a flame-thrower.

Bruce Feirstein

The problem with people who have no vices is that generally you can be pretty sure they're going to have some pretty annoying virtues.

Elizabeth Taylor

When Bob Arum pats you on the back, he's just looking for a spot in which to stick the knife in.

Cus D'Amato

Memorial services are the cocktail parties of the geriatric set.

Ralph Richardson

If you want to look young and thin, hang around with old fat people.

Jim Eason

Why do most forms of swearing involve deities or genitals?

Jerry Seinfeld

Never buy a pit bull terrier from a one-armed man.

Dan Thompson

For sincere personal advice and the correct time, phone any number at random at 3 am.

Steve Martin

The advantage of the emotions is that they lead us astray.

Oscar Wilde

If your boss gets drunk and offers to photocopy her posterior, do not helpfully suggest pressing 'reduce 75%'.

Scott Adams

I like to do the talking myself, it saves time and prevents arguments.

Oscar Wilde

Social Behaviour...

Some people's idea of free speech is that they are free to say anything they like, but if anyone says anything back, that is an outrage.

Winston Churchill

Don't take advice from people with missing fingers.

Henry Beard

I used to laugh at my dog: like marking out his territory was really going to keep those other dogs away. But since I started doing it myself, I have to admit that my co-workers seldom come into my cubicle any more.

John Murphy

One of the lessons of history is that nothing is often a good thing to do and always a clever thing to say.

Will Durant

I would have thought that the knowledge that you are going to be leapt upon by half-a-dozen congratulatory, but sweaty team-mates would be inducement not to score a goal.

Arthur Marshall

Let's banish bridge. Let's find some pleasant way of being miserable together.

Don Herold

One should never listen. To listen is a sign of indifference to one's hearers.

Oscar Wilde

Evelyn Waugh looked like a letter delivered to the wrong address.

Malcolm Muggeridge

No gentleman ever has any money and no gentleman ever takes exercise.

Oscar Wilde

The true spirit of Christmas is people being helped by people other than me.

Jerry Seinfeld

She is always very nice to her inferiors, whenever she can find them.

Dorothy Parker

The view from a hotel room is immaterial, except to the hotelier, who of course charges it on the bill. A gentleman never looks out of the window.

Oscar Wilde

Never underestimate the power of stupid people in large groups.

George Carlin

Sometimes I wonder if I'm patriotic enough. Yes, I want to kill people, but on both sides.

Jack Handey

You've got to take the bitter with the sour.

Samuel Goldwyn

A fellow who is always declaring he's no fool usually has his suspicions...

Wilson Mizner

A lady said to me that I must remember her because she had met me with Douglas Fairbanks. I replied that I didn't even remember Douglas Fairbanks.

Noël Coward

There is nobody so irritating as somebody with less intelligence and more sense than we have.

Don Herold

Is there a justifiable link between good manners and one person necessarily paying for the whole evening just because they are possessed of a Y chromosome?

Neil Cooper

I went and tried to have a trendy haircut and now I look like a lesbian on the female tennis circuit.

Hugh Grant

I wouldn't say I invented tack, but I definitely brought it to its present high popularity.

Bette Midler

Never pick your nose when you're working with superglue.

Emo Philips

Social Behaviour...

Every man reaps what he sows in this life – except the amateur gardener.

Lesley Hall

No civilised person ever goes to bed the day he gets up.

Richard Davis

The wise are polite all the world over, but only fools are polite at home.

Oliver Goldsmith

At times of crisis I find extravagance sometimes helps me.

Robert Morley

It is always a silly thing to give advice, but to give good advice is absolutely fatal.

Oscar Wilde

W. C. Fields never wanted to hurt anybody. He just felt an obligation.

Gregory LaCava

Clubs are mausoleums of inactive masculinity for men who prefer armchairs to women.

V. S. Pritchett

Details are always vulgar.

Oscar Wilde

'O, for an axe!' my soul cries out in railway stations, 'to hew limb from limb all the friends and Jezebels between me and the ticket office.'

Logan Pearsall Smith

I never make the same mistake twice. I always make new ones.

Mary Kenny

I'm all in favour of free expression provided it is kept rigidly under control.

Alan Bennett

If a man is going to behave like a bastard, he had better be a genius.

Jill Craigie

Don Rickles must be smart. He's insulted everyone around and he still has his teeth.

George Burns

When a woman is wearing shorts, her charms are enlarged without being enhanced.

Beverley Nichols

Telling lies is a fault in a boy, an art in a lover, an accomplishment in a bachelor and second nature in a married woman.

Helen Rowland

Sport

With Ron Yeats at centre-half, we could play Arthur Askey in goal.

Bill Shankly

I'm hitting the woods just great, but I'm having a terrible time getting out of them.

Harry Toscano

The only advice my caddy gave me was to keep my putts low.

Lee Trevino

Just as the Wimbledon umpire called 'New balls please', a male streaker dived over the net and did a forward roll on the court.

Elizabeth Judge

Are there bunkers in St Andrew's?

Tiger Woods

All professional athletes are bilingual. They speak English and profanity.

Gordie Howe

I love women – my mother is a woman.

Mike Tyson

A lot of horses get distracted – it's just human nature.

Nick Zito

Football is not a contact sport; it is a collision sport. Dancing is a contact sport.

Vince Lombardi

I've read my husband David Beckham's autobiography from cover to cover. It's got some nice pictures.

'Posh Spice'

I have to exercise in the morning before my brain figures out what I'm doing.

Marsha Doble

After the Royal Command Performance, I asked the Queen if she was keen on football. When she replied that she was not very keen, I asked her if I could have her cup final tickets.

Tommy Cooper

He waltzed through the defence like a magician and shot like Tommy Cooper.

Len Shackleton

I think I was the best baseball player I ever saw.

Willie Mays

The racecourse is as level as a billiard ball.

John Francombe

Strangely, in the slow-motion replay the ball seemed to hang in the air for even longer.

David Acfield

With half the race gone, there is still half the race to go.

Murray Walker

Rugby League is the best sport in the world. It's got everything – speed and tough ugly men.

Terry O'Connor

Cycling is not a sport. It is sado-masochism on a major level.

David Miller

David Beckham cannot kick with his left foot, he cannot head a ball, he cannot tackle and he doesn't score many goals. Apart from that, he's all right.

George Best

Mansell can see him on his earphone.

Murray Walker

I like my baseball players to be married and in debt. That's the way you motivate them.

Ernie Banks

An oxymoron is when two contradictory concepts are juxtaposed such as in 'footballing brain'.

Patrick Murray

I bought a greyhound the other day. I'm going to race it. And by the look of it, I think I'd beat it.

Tommy Cooper

The new sliding roof on Wembley Stadium is designed to keep Gareth Southgate penalties in.

Angus Deayton

Well, either side could win it, or it could be a draw.

Ron Atkinson

The lead car is absolutely unique, except for the one behind it which is identical.

Murray Walker

If it doesn't fart or eat hay, my daughter isn't interested in it.

The Duke of Edinburgh

Apart from their three goals to our one, I thought we were the better team.

Jimmy Quinn

So many English football players go abroad and spend all their time in hotel rooms booking airline tickets and mainlining Marmite.

Simon Barnes

If you can't be an athlete, be an athletic supporter.

Eve Arden

I have been told I am the Nureyev of American football. Who the hell is Nureyev?

Jack Lambert

Sport

I can't imagine what kind of problem Senna has. I imagine it must be some sort of grip problem.

Murray Walker

Am I scared? Of course I'm scared. I'm scared I might kill Schmelling.

Joe Louis

We are going to turn this team around 360 degrees.

Jason Kidd

I was putting like a blind lobotomised baboon.

Tony Johnson

Baseball is 90 per cent mental. The other half is physical.

Yogi Berra

And Damon Hill is coming into the pit lane, yes, it's Damon Hill coming into the Williams pit, and Damon Hill in the pit, no, it's Michael Schumacher.

Murray Walker

I would not say that David Ginola is the best winger in the Premier Division but there is none better.

Ron Atkinson

The three saddest words in the English language: Patrick Thistle, nil.

Billy Connolly

In women's tennis, the Williamses hate the Hingises, the Hingeses hate the Williamses, Davenport hates Mauresmo and everybody hates Kournikova.

Simon Barnes

The entire secret of my success is not to play snooker with a lefthanded Welsh miner.

Ted Ray

I spent all day yesterday wading through streams and dropping hooks into deep water. That's the last time I'm going to waste playing golf.

Tommy Cooper

I think I fail a bit less than everyone else.

Jack Nicklaus

You've got to time your babies for the off-season and get married in the off-season. Baseball always comes first.

Liz Mitchell

In the Bowling alley of Tomorrow, there will even be machines that wear rental shoes and throw the ball for you. Your sole function will be to drink beer.

Dave Barry

We've signed five foreigners over the summer but I'll be on hand to learn them a bit of English.

Denis Wise

If Giles and Clark went to the toilet, I wanted their markers there as well.

Dick Graham

There's a new drink in Glasgow called the Souness. One half and you're off.

Tommy Docherty

George Best is probably a better player than Tom Finney. But you have to remember that Tom is sixty now.

Bill Shankly

There's nothing wrong with the Old Course at St Andrew's that a hundred bulldozers couldn't put right.

Ed Furjol

I don't use a long-handled putter. If I'm going to miss a putt, I want to look good doing it.

Chi Chi Rodriguez

The Irish Rugby Team in my day was all boot, bollock and bite.

Gordon Wood

What do I have to shoot to win the tournament? The rest of the field.

Roger Maltbie

Essentially my caddie has been retired since he was 21.

Jack Nicklaus

Sammy Davis Jr hits the ball 130 yards and his jewelry goes 150 yards.

Bob Hope

A Manchester City fan is a man who hates his wife so much he will use any excuse to get out of the house.

Bernard Manning

On the fifteenth at Royal Birkdale, we put down my bag to hunt for a ball; we found the ball but lost the bag.

Lee Trevino

My wife says that if I don't give up golf, she'll leave me. I'm really going to miss her.

Eric Morecambe

Queen's Park against Forfar – you can't get more romantic than that.

Archie MacPherson

What is my advice to a struggling golfer? Take two weeks off and then quit the game.

Jimmy Demaret

The sign of a good golfer is a tan like mine. It tells you the player is spending a lot of time out on the fairway and the greens and not in the trees.

Lee Trevino

Sport

For Manchester United to get a penalty, we need a certificate from the Pope and a personal letter from the Queen.

Alex Ferguson

I get out of breath playing chess.

Ken Dodd

A professional wrestling referee is a great job. You're a referee in a sport with no rules of any kind. How do you screw that up?

Jerry Seinfeld

Some of these legends have been around golf a long time. When they mention a good grip, they're talking about their dentures.

Bob Hope

My doctor warned me to avoid excitement, so now I watch only League of Ireland football matches.

Phillip Green

What do I think of Tiger Woods? I don't know; I've never played there.

Sandy Lyle

Pothitivity begats pothitivity, whereas negativity begats negativity begats negativity. Pleathe, help me with this message.

Chris Eubank

Mothers keep a photograph of the Munster rugby team on the mantelpiece to keep their kids from going too near the fire.

Jim Neilly

Arnold Palmer is the biggest crowd-pleaser since the invention of the portable sanitary facility.

Bob Hope

They wouldn't have won if we had beaten them.

Yogi Berra

At the last Olympic Games some of the winners' samples did a lap of honour.

Ken Dodd

We didn't lose the game – we just ran out of time.

Vince Lombardi

Ian Botham is in no way inhibited by a capacity to over-intellectualise.

Frances Edmonds

We made a lot of wrong mistakes.

Yogi Berra

Chess is a foolish expedient for making idle people believe they are doing something very clever when they are only wasting their time.

George Bernard Shaw

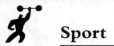

Sport

A football game is more like an emergency happening at a distance than a sport.

Jacques Barzun

A British rowing eight – eight minds with but a single thought – if that.

Max Beerbohm

Tom Finney had the opposition so frightened that they had a man marking him when they were warming up before the kick-off.

Bill Shankly

The referee was booking everyone. I thought he was filling in his Lottery numbers.

Ian Wright

I'm throwing just as hard as I ever did. The ball's just not getting there as fast.

Vernon Gomez

If swimming is good for your figure, how do you explain whales?

Lily Tomlin

David Beckham has two feet, which a lot of players do not have nowadays.

Jimmy Hill

Think only of two things in athletics – the gun and the tape. When you hear the one, just run like hell until you break the other.

Sam Mussabini

'Play it as it lies' is one of the fundamental dictates of golf. The other is 'Wear it if it clashes.'

Henry Beard

I hit him mostly in the face because I felt sorry for his family and thought I would select the only place that couldn't be disfigured.

Mike Leonard

The depressing thing about tennis is that no matter how good you get, you'll never be as good as a wall.

Mitch Hedberg

When I got through with him he was all covered in blood – my blood.

Jimmy Durante

Football's a game of skill – we kicked them a bit and they kicked us a bit.

Graham Roberts

I played golf the other day and shot a birdie. The little bastard wouldn't stop tweeting while I was trying to putt.

Mitch Murray

There is only one thing in the world dumber than playing golf and that is watching someone else playing golf.

Peter Andres

That's a wise substitution by Terry Venables – three fresh men, three fresh legs.

Jimmy Hill

Any persons (except players) caught collecting golf balls on this course will be prosecuted and have their balls removed.

Michael Mavor

I've never lost a golf ball – I've never hit one far enough to lose one.

Bob Hope

Look at Stephen Hendry sitting there totally focused just staring into space.

David Vine

I missed Nicky Perez with some tremendous punches. The wind alone from them could have caused him pneumonia.

Barry McGuigan

Di Matteo's taken to playing in midfield like a duck out of water.

Peter Osgood

Women have but one task in sport, that of crowning the winner with garlands.

Baron De Coubertin

If you can't beat them, arrange to have them beaten.

George Clooney

If Clough was Van Hooijdonk's manager, he'd be suspended – from a roof beam.

Ron Atkinson

Germany are a very difficult team to play. They had eleven internationals out there today.

Steve Lomas

Nobody cares if Le Saux is gay or not. It is the fact that he openly reads the *Guardian* that makes him the most reviled man in football.

Piers Morgan

The world may be divided into people who read, people who write and fox hunters.

William Shenstone

Nothing increases your golf score like witnesses.

Bob Hope

You guys pair up in groups of three, then line up in a circle.

Bill Peterson

We can't win at home. We can't win away. As manager, I just can't figure out where else to play.

Pat Williams

Theatre and Criticism

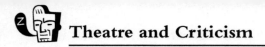

Last year I was voted the best ventriloquist in Britain – by the British Lipreaders' Association.

David Dixon

You have to admire Madonna. She hides her lack of talent so well.

Manolo Blahnik

When I saw Dylan Thomas's *Under Milk Wood* on television, I thought that the best thing in the programme was the 20-minute breakdown.

George Murray

Your play is delightful, and there's nothing that can't be fixed.

Gertrude Lawrence

I saw 'Midsummer Night's Dream', which I had never seen before nor shall ever see again, for it is the most insipid, ridiculous play ever I saw in my life.

Samuel Pepys

I'm very proud of you. You managed to play the first act of *Blithe Spirit* tonight with all the Chinese flair and light–hearted brilliance of Lady Macbeth.

Noël Coward

George Bernard Shaw was the first man to have cut a swathe through the theatre and left it strewn with virgins.

Frank Harris

As a comedian I've got a lot of laughs – but mostly in bed.

Steve Martin

You can't accept one individual's criticism, particularly if the critic is female: when they get their period it's difficult for them to function as normal human beings.

Jerry Lewis

I'm not the first straight dancer or the last.

Mikhail Baryshnikov

Some directors couldn't direct lemmings off a cliff.

Doug Brod

I've seen better plots than *Break a Leg* in a cemetery.

Steward Klein

Thank you very much ladies and gentlemen. You've been 50 per cent.

Max Wall

Sarah Bernhardt had a clause in her contract forbidding animal acts to play with her, but she permitted W.C. Fields.

Mae West

June Whitfield has supported more actors than the Department of Health and Social Security.

Barry Took

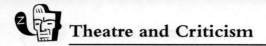

I regret to say that 'scrota' is an anagram of 'actors'.

John Gielgud

At least one of my children did one of my plays at A–level. I think he got a 'B' with my help.

Tom Stoppard

I like to be introduced as America's foremost actor. It saves the necessity of further effort.

John Barrymore

When you're hot, casting directors say: The part is actually for a midget but we think you're perfect for it. But when you're cold they'll say: Michael, we're doing the Michael Caine Story, but unfortunately you're a bit too short.

Michael Caine

He's the only director whose plays close on the first day of rehearsal.

Mel Brooks

O God, send me some good actors – cheap.

Lilian Baylis

They gave me a present of Mornington Crescent – they threw it a brick at a time.

W. F. Hargreaves

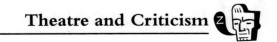

There comes a sad and bewildering moment in the life of every actress when you are no longer the cherished darling, but must turn the corner and try to be funny.

Billy Burke

Viewed as drama, the First World War was somewhat disappointing.

D. W. Griffith

Why didn't Jack Benny hit a home run like I told him to? If he's not going to do what I tell him to do, what's the use of my being manager of the actors' baseball team?

Groucho Marx

My dear chap! Good isn't the word for your performance.

W. S. Gilbert

Kenneth Tynan said I had only two gestures, the left hand up, the right hand up. What did he want me to do, bring out my prick?

John Gielgud

Most actors are latent homosexuals and we cover it with drink.

Richard Burton

Dear Ingrid Bergman – speaks five languages and can't act in any of them.

John Gielgud

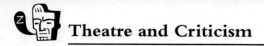

If Lear had been given electric shocks, there would have been no need for all that nonsense.

R. D. Laing

Style for an actor is knowing which play you're in.

John Gielgud

I always had one ear offstage, listening for the call from the bookie.

Walter Matthau

Sherard Blaw, the dramatist who had discovered himself and who gave so ungrudgingly of his discovery to the world.

Saki

I have never played the Glasgow Empire. I am a comedian, not a missionary.

Max Miller

Pinero's eyebrows are like the skins of some small mammal just not large enough to be used as mats.

Max Beerbohm

A character actor is one who cannot act and therefore makes an elaborate study of disguise and stage tricks by which acting can be grotesquely simulated.

George Bernard Shaw

The play had only one fault. It was kind of lousy.

James Thurber

Like his contemporary, Ben Elton, Harry Enfield probably needs to move into new territory – Azerbaijan perhaps, or Tierra Del Fuego.

Paul Hoggart

An audience is never wrong. An individual member of it may be an imbecile, but a thousand imbeciles together in the dark – that's critical genius.

Billy Wilder

A good actor must never be in love with anyone except himself.

Jean Anouilh

Very few people go to the doctor when they have a cold. They go to the theatre instead.

Boyd Gatewood

What do you expect me to do if nobody writes good plays any more and we are reduced to putting on plays by Pirandello?

Luigi Pirandello

A drama critic is a man who leaves no turn unstoned.

George Bernard Shaw

The cast of this play is not as strong as the one in the leading lady's left eye.

Jimmy Cairncross

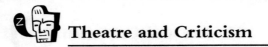

Frank Harris is upstairs thinking about Shakespeare at the top of his voice.

Oscar Wilde

Actors are people who never give their right age except in time of war.

Paula Victor

I know exactly why I got the London Critics' Award. They thought 'Harris lives in the Savoy, so he'll just roll out of bed and be here in two seconds. No taxis, no planes, no expenses.'

Richard Harris

I didn't pay £3.50 just to see half a dozen acorns and a chipolata.

Noel Coward

The last time Bertie Ahern went to the theatre was when they attempted – and failed – to remove his adenoids.

Hugh Leonard

My bust was visible under a negligee in one scene. Suddenly I was worried that people might concentrate on my body instead of on my acting.

Barbra Streisand

I used to lie about being an actor and tell taxi drivers that I was an electrician.

John Gordon-Sinclair

Theatre and Criticism

King Lear was a strange horrible business, but I suppose good enough for Shakespeare's day.

Queen Victoria

Daddy, when I grow up I want to be an actor.
Don't be greedy, son, you can't be both.

Hugh Leonard

The trouble with crocodiles as dramatic actors is that they have only one facial expression.

John Cleese

My ad-libs aren't worth the paper they're written on.

Bob Hope

As a comedian I have wonderful timing – I always get to the back door before the audience does.

Ken Dodd

It shouldn't make a hair's breadth of a difference to an actor if he has a dead baby at home and a wife dying.

Cedric Hardwicke

Noël Coward was monocle of all he surveyed.

Kenneth Tynan

Am I with the show? Well, let's say I'm not against it.

George S. Kaufman

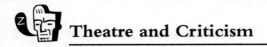

Age shall not wither her, nor iron bars a cage.

Kenneth Williams

In every play of Ibsen's, a stranger comes into the room, opens a window to let in fresh air and everyone dies of pneumonia.

Somerset Maugham

Has anybody ever seen a dramatic critic in the daytime? Of course not. They come out after dark, up to no good.

P. G. Wodehouse

Let's play horse. I'll be the front end and you play yourself.

Les Dawson

Sergeant, arrest several of those vicars.

Philip King

Giving Clive Barnes the CBE for services to the theatre was like giving Goering the DSO for services to the RAF.

Alan Bennett

The only objection to 'The Forgotten Factor' I see is that it makes people smile all the time, which gives a suggestion of harmless idiocy.

Beverley Baxter

The performance of *The Three Musketeers* was Athos, Pathos and Bathos.

Oscar Wilde

What a house attended my performance the other night. I've seen more at the Moscow Conservative Club.

Les Dawson

I once visited the House of Terror, or, as I prefer to call it, the Glasgow Empire.

Ken Dodd

Doris, the audience are not actually hissing you; it's just a lot of people whispering to each other, 'That's Doris Cooper, Gladys Cooper's sister.'

Noel Coward

At no point in the performance of *Good Mourning Mrs Brown* is Brendan O'Carroll in danger of becoming two–dimensional.

John McKeowan

Miss Davies has just two expressions – joy and indigestion.

James Agate

John Gielgud's grace and poise are remarkable and his voice would melt the entire Inland Revenue.

James Agate

When I asked the director how the Shakespeare was coming along he told me it was Ibsen. I reminded him that it was all costume.

Lew Grade

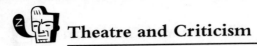

The show must go on, or don't give them back their money under any circumstances is the first principle of theatrical management.

Robert Morley

I've known some actors who were intelligent, but the better the actor, the more stupid he is.

Truman Capote

Most of the cast gave performances which looked as if they had been recruited from the rejects of the annual pantomime in a backward village.

Robert Morley

The theatre got along very nicely without directors for approximately 2535 years.

Walter Kerr

I like the lights full up all the time, but will allow imaginative directors to keep them low until I burst into view, after which the rule, if I am allowed to make it, is light, light and still more light.

Robert Morley

Claudette Colbert knew her lines in *Blithe Spirit* backwards. And that's exactly the way she delivered them.

Noël Coward

Don't worry, you'll survive. No one dies in the middle of Act Five.

Henrik Ibsen

Show business is like sex – you need a good start and a big finish.

George Burns

Milton Berle, Bob Hope, Henny Youngman – those kids will do fine.

George Burns

The word 'hypocrisy' is derived from the Greek word for actor.

Frederic Raphael

Norma Shearer had a face always splendidly unclouded by thought.

Lillian Hellman

Rex Harrison's greatest trick was as he left the stage to start a round of applause in the wings which it was hoped the audience would duly pick up and echo to the rafters.

Sheridan Morley

House Beautiful is play lousy.

Dorothy Parker

An actor is a guy who takes a girl in his arms, looks tenderly into her eyes, and tells her how great he is.

S. J. Perelman

Shaw's plays are the price we pay for Shaw's prefaces.

James Agate

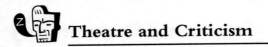

Have you seen my Bottom? They say it's my best part.

John Gielgud

Critics are remembered only by what they failed to understand.

George Moore

Directors are such useful fellows. They take your coat in the morning and hand it back at the end of rehearsal.

Wilfrid Hyde-White

Let Shakespeare do it his way, I'll do it mine. We'll see who comes out better.

Mae West

Miscellaneous

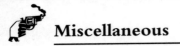 **Miscellaneous**

A special evacuation medal should be presented to all
survivors of the Crete campaign. It should be inscribed
simply EX CRETA.

> Evelyn Waugh

Queen Victoria is more of a man than I expected.

> Henry James

How is it that the first piece of luggage on the airport
carousel never belongs to anyone?

> George Roberts

The first rule of comedy is not to perform in a town where
they still point at aeroplanes.

> Bobby Mills

On one occasion I drove a car into the wall of my house
which failed to take evasive action.

> John Mortimer

Soldiers who wish to be a hero
Are practically zero.
But those who wish to be civilians
Jesus they run into millions.

> Norman Rosten

It is not a bomb; it is a device which is exploding.

> Jacques Le Blanc

At Houdini's funeral I bet a hundred bucks that he wasn't in the coffin.

Charles Dillingham

Most of us know instinctively that the phrase 'trust me, light this fuse' is a recipe for disaster.

Wendy Northcutt

The most dangerous thing in a combat zone is an officer with a map.

Patrick Murray

Captain Hook died because he wiped with the wrong hand.

Tommy Sledge

He had a fine head of dandruff.

Spike Milligan

Wife unable to obtain bidet for shipment from Paris. Suggest handstand in shower.

Billy Wilder

Being a hero is one of the shortest–lived professions there is.

Will Rogers

If we lose this war, I'll start another in my wife's name.

Moshe Dayan

 **Miscellaneous**

Courage is often lack of insight, whereas cowardice in many cases is based on good information.

Peter Ustinov

It is time for the human race to enter the solar system.

Dan Quayle

In response to a holiday query, I received the following reply: 'Standing among savage scenery, the hotel offers stupendous revelations. There is a French widow in every bedroom, affording delightful prospects.'

Gerard Hoffnung

Every night for the last eight years I've sat in my house staring at the rug trying to move it by telekinesis. It hasn't moved an inch. But the house is gone.

Steven Wright

It gets late early out here.

Yogi Berra

I have just read in your magazine that I am dead. Don't forget to delete me from your list of subscribers.

Rudyard Kipling

This guy came up to me in the street and said, 'Do you mind if I ask you a question?' I said to him 'Didn't give me much of a choice there buddy, did you?'

Steven Wright

I met Colonel House, the great little man who can be silent in several languages.

James Harbord

The results of psychology experiments apply only to the participants – first-year college psychology students.

Patrick Murray

I like to skydive horizontally.

Steven Wright

Mrs Santa Claus is very upset because her husband has a list of the names of all the really bad girls.

Robin Williams

If you tell a joke in the forest, but nobody laughs, was it a joke?

Steven Wright

It doesn't beggar well for the future.

Henry McLeish

Have you noticed that all hot-water bottles look like Henry the Eighth?

Max Beerbohm

If you can't imitate him, don't copy him.

Yogi Berra

Miscellaneous

It was a three-star hotel – I could see them through the roof.

Frankie Howard

I started using Grecian 2000 and now I look like a 2000-year-old Greek.

Roy Brown

Airplane travel is Nature's way of making you look like your passport photograph.

Al Gore

Whose cruel idea was it for the word 'lisp' to have an 's' in it?

Chris Maude

In the army I joined the Tank Corps because I preferred to go into battle sitting down.

Peter Ustinov

Put procrastination off until tomorrow.

Steven Wright

I picked up the phone and said, 'Is this the local swimming baths?' A voice said, 'That all depends where you're ringing from.'

Tommy Cooper

I always wear battledress. It is practical, simple, cheap and does not go out of fashion.

Fidel Castro

Miscellaneous

You can take a horse to water, but a pencil must be lead.

Stan Laurel

Wars teach us not to love our enemies but to hate our allies.

W. L. George

Don't use shampoo – use the real thing.

Rodney Dangerfield

His eminence was due to the flatness of the surrounding landscape.

John Stuart Mill

A tombstone is the only thing that can stand upright and lie on its face at the same time.

Mary Little

Ferdinand Foch is just a frantic pair of moustaches.

T. E. Lawrence

Never get yourself into a position where the only escape route is vertically upwards.

George Patton

Why do they lock gas station bathrooms? Are they afraid someone will clean them?

Jerry Seinfeld

Miscellaneous

No man is an island, but six men bound together make quite an effective raft.

Jo Brand

The models were so nervous backstage they were keeping their food down.

Jack Dee

You know something? Dogs go through life and they never have any money. Not a cent! And do you know why? No pockets.

Jerry Seinfeld

I don't dance, but I'd love to hold you while you do.

Leslie Phillips

The bowling ball is the natural enemy of the egg.

Michael Davis

According to most studies, people's number one fear is public speaking. Number two is death.

Jerry Seinfeld

Jeremy Clarkson claims to be able to tell the make of car he is driving while blindfolded.

A. A. Gill

I've been accused of being a fatalist, but I've never collected a postage stamp in my life.

Yogi Berra

Miscellaneous

Imagine if there were no hypothetical situations.

John Mendosa

I've often wondered, do kippers swim folded or flat?

Ken Dodd

Matt Busby was the eternal optimist. In 1968 he still hoped Glenn Miller was just missing.

Pat Crerand

A legend is a lie that has attained the dignity of age.

H. L. Mencken

I don't give a damn what colour you are so long as you get out there and kill those sonsofbitches in green suits.

George S. Patton

We who are about to die are going to take one hell of a lot of bastards with us.

Joel Rosenberg

Something tells me that they probably screwed up and named Murphy's Law after the wrong guy.

Doug Finney

We are not retreating – we are merely advancing another direction.

Douglas Adams

Miscellaneous

The most merciful thing in the world is the inability of the human mind to correlate all its contents.

H. P. Lovecraft

First things first, but not necessarily in that order.

Steven Wright

If the garbage man calls, tell him we don't want any.

Groucho Marx

Don't count your chickens before they cross the road.

Steven Wright

It's cheaper to have your horn made louder than to have your brakes repaired.

George Burns

I went to see a psychiatrist. He said, 'Tell me everything.' I did and now he's doing my act.

Henny Youngman

It's no longer a sin to be rich, it's a miracle.

James Simpson

Boy am I annoyed tonight – I spent an hour blow-drying my hair and then I forgot to bring it with me.

George Burns

I feel great and I kiss even better.

Emo Philips

Why should I fill in a census form? I spent ages filling it in last time and I didn't win a thing.

Giles Coren

I once built a ship in a bottle. They had to break the bottle to let me out.

Steven Wright

A man loses his dog so he puts an ad in the paper. The ad says 'Here boy.'

Spike Milligan

Any fool can do lion–taming and only a fool does.

Robert Morley

Don't use that foreign word ideals. We have that excellent native word lies.

Henry Ibsen

If you keep saying things are going to be bad, you have the chance of becoming a prophet.

Isaac Singer

A toastmaster is a man who eats a meal he doesn't want so he can get up and tell a lot of stories he doesn't remember to people who've already heard them.

George Jessel

Miscellaneous

You can say any foolish thing to a dog, and the dog will give you a look that says, 'My God, you're right! I never would have thought of that!'

Sean Connery

They all laughed at Joan of Arc but she didn't care. She went right ahead and built it.

Gracie Allen

I was in the Intelligence Corps in the Army in the desert. I was so short and my bum was so near the ground it always wiped out my footprints. Nobody could ever find me.

Harry Secombe

Aim for the moon and you can reach the stars.

Peter Beardsley

Born with a withered arm, the Kaiser continually tried to demonstrate his manliness. One of his hobbies was chopping down whole plantations of trees with a special axe.

Roger Boyes

You're just jealous because the voices talk only to me.

Emo Philips

The best gift for a man who has everything is encouragement, penicillin or a burglar alarm.

Joan Rivers

I've cut it twice and it's still too short.

Gracie Allen

Index

Index

Acfield, David 265
Acheson, Dean 213
Ackroyd, Dan 127
Ackroyd, Peter 93
Adams, Douglas 44, 301
Adams, Franklin P. 45, 91
Adams, Joey 231
Adams, Scott 25, 146, 242, 256
Adams, Tony 45
Adashek, Jonathan 108
Ade, George 244
Aesop 201
Agate, James 27, 79, 141, 289, 290
Agee, James 141
Aitken, Jonathan 51
Alda, Alan 33
Aldrin, Buzz 226
Aleichem, Sholem 33
Alexander, Alistair 194
Alexander, Hilary 18
Allen, Dave 205, 221
Allen, Fred 33
Allen, Gracie 60, 66, 67, 89, 109, 157, 304
Allen, Steve 162
Allen, Woody 32, 55, 57, 73, 136, 151, 183, 228, 230, 237, 238
Alsop, Joseph 200
Altman, Steve 39
Amin, Idi 246
Amis, Kingsley 43, 98, 182
Amis, Martin 197
Amory, Cleveland 109
Andres, Peter 276
Andrews, Paul 228, 231
Annan, Lord 49
Anouilh, Jean 285
Arbeiter, Karl 236
Archer, George 76
Arden, Eve 267
Armour, Richard 100

Armstrong, Louis 217
Armstrong, Morey 165
Armstrong, Robert 202
Arnold, David 226
Arnold, Matthew 191
Asimov, Isaac 237
Asquith, Margot 159, 209
Astor, Mary 135
Astor, Nancy 219
Atkinson, Ron 146, 173, 267, 268, 277
Attenborough, Richard 202
Aubrey, John 156
Auden, W. H. 89

Bagehot, Walter 210
Baker, Eric W. 189
Baker, James 205
Baker, Richard 194
Baker, Russell 238
Balfour, A. J. 89
Ball, Peter 191
Ballesteros, Seve 48
Bankhead, Tallulah 16, 49, 141
Banks, Ernie 266
Barbi, Shane 134
Barbirolli, John 175
Barclay, Michael 174
Barnes, Simon 267, 269
Barr, Roseanne 65, 115, 117, 161, 175, 218
Barres, Maurice 207
Barrett, Elizxabeth 252
Barrie, J. M. 125, 253
Barry, Dave 13, 17, 26, 40, 41, 62, 73, 74, 99, 102, 103, 110, 113, 169, 196, 214, 228, 229, 231, 232, 233, 237, 239, 269
Barrymore, John 92, 282
Bart Simpson 75
Barzan, Gerald 25

Index

Barzun, Jacques 274
Baskin, Leonard 15
Bateson, Dingwall 72
Baughman, Dale 103
Baxter, Anne 253
Baxter, Beverley 288
Baylis, Lilian 282
Bean, Orson 145
Beard, Henry 68, 257, 275
Beardsley, Peter 304
Beckham, David 216
Beckham, Victoria 265
Beecham, Thomas 168, 175, 182
Beerbohm, Max 83, 90, 274, 284, 297
Behan, Brendan 188, 194, 244, 249
Behan, Dominic 218
Bell, Ian 38
Benbow, John 92
Benchley, Robert 44, 90
Bennett, Alan 92, 124, 261, 288
Bennett, Dan 124
Bennett, James 141
Benny, Jack 130
Bentley, Dick 102
Berk, Ronald 85
Berle, Milton 26, 101, 126, 137
Berne, Eric 155
Bernstein, Robert 55
Bernstein, Sheryl 25
Berra, Yogi 32, 144, 268, 273, 296, 297, 300
Best, George 38, 266
Betts, Hannah 105
Bevin, Ernest 97, 202
Bhoy, Danny 39, 181
Bierce, Ambrose 42, 49, 68, 69, 84, 89, 104, 163, 173, 210, 220
Billings, Josh 32, 45, 54, 104, 160, 220
Binder, Mike 113, 254

Bing, Rudolph 168
Bishop, William 19
Bitel, Nick 164
Blahnik, Manolo 280
Blair, Tony 213
Bliss, Lara 54
Blount, Roy 13
Bluestone, Ed 235
Bogart, Humphrey 139
Bolitho, William 182
Bombeck, Erma 64, 67, 99, 102, 105, 117
Bonaparte, Napoleon 124
Bond, Edward 195
Bone, James 148
Boosler, Elayne 130
Boren, Jim 154
Boswell, James 85
Botham, Ian 53
Boulton, Adam 242
Bowra, Maurice 116
Boyes, Roger 304
Boyle, Andrew 228
Boynton, Sandra 66
Bradbury, Robert 106
Bradley, Chris 62
Brand, Jo 63, 65, 68, 99, 103, 116, 121, 156, 162, 201, 300
Brando, Marlon 218
Branson, Richard 26
Braude, Jacob 189
Brecht, Bertolt 35
Brenan, Gerald 83
Briers, Richard 243
Briffault, Robert 56
Brod, Doug 281
Brodie, John 29
Brookner, Anita 147
Brooks, Mel 87, 217, 282
Brown, Arnold 120
Brown, Chubby 98

Brown, John 52
Brown, Rita Mae 12
Brown, Roy 66, 121, 125, 127, 128, 161, 212, 298
Brummel, Beau 252
Bryson, Bill 87, 185
Buchan, John 222
Buckley, William F. 195
Burchill, Julie 17, 134
Burd, David 143
Burgen, Stephen 40, 245, 249
Burgess, Tony 61
Burke, Billy 283
Burns, George 31, 34, 53, 69, 77, 96, 127, 130, 131, 151, 152, 173, 190, 222, 223, 239, 243, 261, 290, 302
Burns, John 208
Burton, Richard 283
Bush, George W. 24, 34, 56, 97, 190, 204
Butler, Samuel 114, 126, 212
Buttons, Red 96
Byatt, A. S. 110
Byrne, Jason 155
Byron 250

Caen, Herb 61
Caine, Michael 282
Cairncross, Jimmy 285
Callow, Simon 136
Cameron, James 138
Campbell, Roy 83
Cannon, Jimmy 253
Capek, Karel 222
Capote, Truman 144, 290
Capp, Al 193
Capra, Frank 233
Carlin, George 44, 78, 162, 221, 258
Carlyle, Jane 242
Carpenter, Humphrey 87
Carr, Barbara 200

Carroll, Arthur 230
Carson, Frank 114, 191
Carson, Johnny 184, 212
Carter, Billy 42, 105
Carter, Lillian 102
Cartland, Barbara 64
Cashman, Derek 165
Cashman, Peter 234
Castro, Fidel 298
Cau, Jean 238
Cecil, Mary 32
Chandler, Raymond 74
Chaplin, Charlie 217
Charles II, King 74
Chase, Angela 54
Chekhov, Anton 123
Chesterfield, Lord 64
Chesterton, G. K. 54, 247
Child, Julia 65
Chilton, Edward 237
Chisholm, Scott 213
Christenson, Gary 117
Churchill, Randolph 249
Churchill, Winston 48, 200, 204, 209, 211, 250, 257
Ciardi, John 52
Cicero 86, 189
Clancy, Tom 84, 136
Clare, Lord 78
Clark, George 227
Clarke, Kenneth 165, 207
Clarkson, Jeremy 38, 114, 142, 143, 157, 180, 231
Cleese, John 62, 287
Clinton, Bill 145
Clooney, George 277
Clunes, Martin 131
Cohn, Roy 74
Coleridge, Samuel Taylor 223
Coles, Joanna 67, 72
Colette 64

Collins, Phil 114
Condon, Antoine 160
Congreve, William 115
Conley, Brian 129
Connelly, Mary 168
Connery, Sean 304
Connolly, Billy 24, 40, 268
Connolly, Cyril 17
Connor, William 69
Conway, Diane 128, 238
Cook, Carole 67
Cooke, Alistair 115
Cooper, Duff 235
Cooper, Neil 259
Cooper, Tommy 17, 63, 69, 122,
    156, 188, 265, 266, 269, 298
Cope, Wendy 115
Copeland, Bill 147
Copeland, Faye 251
Coren, Alan 88
Coren, Giles 303
Cornford, Francis 49
Cosby, Bill 27, 50, 100, 110
Costello, Lou 115
Cowan, Tam 35
Coward, Noël 91, 169, 259, 280,
    286, 289, 290
Cox, Marcelene 108
Craigie, Jill 261
Crawford, Joan 143
Crerand, Pat 301
Crisp, Quentin 162
Cronenberg, David 231
Crowe, William 209
Crystal, Billy 151
Cummins, Danny 171
Cuppy, Will 251
Curtis, Jamie Lee 49
Cytron, Sara 72

Dalglish, Kenny 191

Dali, Salvador 13
D'Amato, Cus 255
Dangerfield, Rodney 32, 102, 112,
    116, 118, 154, 159, 299
Danson, Ted 126
Darrow, Clarence 55
Davidson, Harley 32
Davidson, Simon 234
Davies, Alan 77, 78, 147
Davies, Bob 43
Davies, Geoffrey 189
Davies, Robertson 86
Davino, Sal 160
Davis, Andrew 151
Davis, Angela 203
Davis, Bette 248
Davis, Michael 300
Davis, Peter 207
Davis, Richard 260
Dawson, Les 66, 74, 107, 108, 124,
    127, 154, 192, 193, 245, 288, 289
Dayan, Moshe 295
De Coubertin, Baron 276
De Mille, Cecil B. 84
De Mondeville, Henri 158
De Vries, Peter 56, 227
Dean, Jay 65
Deayton, Angus 267
DeBarri, Girald 183
Debussy, Claude 169
Dee, Jack 300
Demaret, Jimmy 271
Demetriadis, Mary 255
Depardieu, Gerard 114
Desmond, Barry 201
Deutsch, Adolph 149
Dickens, Charles 72, 112, 173, 191
Dickey, James 84
Dickson, Paul 48
Dickson, Rhonda 119
Diller, Phyllis 29, 78, 105, 112, 119,

128, 154, 218, 255
Dillingham, Charles 295
Dimmet, Ernest 12
Disraeli, Benjamin 209
Dixon, David 280
Dixon, John 27
Dixon, Lee 110
Doble, Marsha 265
Dobler, Conrad 161
Docherty, Tommy 159, 270
Dodd, Ken 31, 106, 107, 108, 125, 172, 174, 190, 235, 272, 273, 287, 289, 301
Dodds, Bill 73
Dole, Bob 231
Donaldson, Sam 214
Douglas, Michael 141
Douglas, Norman 79
Dowdy, Lori 65
Drummond, John 21
Duke of Edinburgh 267
Duncan, Sara 251
Dunn, Nora 162
Dunne, Finley Peter 63, 97
Durant, Will 257
Durante, Jimmy 275

Eason, Jim 256
Eclair, Jenny 97, 155, 229
Eco, Umberto 227
Edinburgh, Duke of 267
Edison, Thomas 234
Edmonds, Frances 273
Edwards, M. G. 246
Elliot, Jimmy 220
Emerson, Ralph Waldo 195
Erasmus, Desiderius 218
Ettinger, Bob 117
Eubank, Chris 89, 272
Evans, Edith 20
Evans, Linda 129

Evans, Nigel 146
Evarts, William 39
Everage, Edna 251
Ewing, Winnie 203

Fadiman, Clifton 82
Farr, Charles 242
Faulkner, William 40, 92
Feather, William 159
Fechtner, Leopald 101
Feherty, David 254
Feirstein, Bruce 255
Ferguson, Alex 272
Ferguson, Sarah 34, 125, 159
Feynman, Richard 53, 230, 236
Fields, Totie 66
Fields, W. C. 38, 39, 40, 41, 43, 44, 46, 114, 125, 182, 245
Figueredo, Joao 213
Finney, Doug 301
Fischer, Martin 157
Fiterman, Linda 119
Flanner, Janet 242
Flowers, Gennifer 134
Floyd, Keith 42
Flynn, Paul 206
Fonda, Henry 138
Ford, Barbara 253
Ford, Harrison 183
Ford, John 142, 146, 147
Forfleet, Susan 162
Fox, Henry 26
Fox, J. R. 253
Foxworthy, Jeff 110
Francombe, John 265
Franklin, Benjamin 76
Frederick the great 194
Freed, Arthur 182
Freud, Sigmund 226
Frostrup, Mariella 247
Furjol, Ed 270

Index

Fuss, Bob 54

Gabor, Zsa Zsa 126, 248
Galbraith, J. K. 32, 76
Galsworthy, John 120
Gandhi, Mahatma 142
Garner, John 205
Gatewood, Boyd 285
Gauss, Carl Friedrich 228
Geneen, Harold 27
George I, King 13
George, W. L. 299
Getty, J. Paul 27, 28
Gibbon, Edward 205
Gibson, Mel 134
Gielgud, John 282, 283, 284, 292
Gilbert, Denise 129
Gilbert, W. S. 77, 171, 212, 283
Giles, Geoffrey 207
Gill, A. A. 144, 226, 300
Gillespie, Dizzy 169
Gladstone, W. E. 93
Glasow, Arnold 108
Glass, Senator 204
Gogarty, Oliver St John 185
Gold, Mary 122
Goldsmith, Oliver 260
Goldwait, Bobcat 147
Goldwyn, Samuel 138, 142, 170,
    171, 258
Gomez, Vernon 274
Gordon, George 88
Gordon-Sinclair, John 286
Gore, Al 211, 298
Grade, Lew 140, 289
Graham, Dick 270
Graham, Laurie 193
Grant, Cary 25
Grant, Hugh 259
Grant, Ulysses S. 195
Graves, Robert 84

Green, Phillip 272
Greene, Graham 140
Greer, Germaine 132
Gregory, Dick 186, 208
Griffith, D. W. 146, 283
Grizzard, Lewis 69, 103
Groening, Matt 235
Grove, Valerie 89
Guftason, John 200
Guinan, Texas 125

Hackett, Buddy 62
Hague, William 207
Haig, Douglas 183
Hailey, Arthur 28
Haldane, J. B. S. 232
Hall, Lesley 260
Hall, Rich 175
Hall, Robin 77
Hamilton, Alex 18
Hampton, Christopher 247
Hancock, Tony 87
Handey, Jack 40, 62, 118, 258
Hanslick, Eduard 176
Hanson, Gerry 124
Harbord, James 297
Harding, Mike 170
Hardwick, Cedric 287
Hargreaves, W. F. 282
Harney, Bill 60
Harris, Frank 280
Harris, George 49
Harris, Richard 286
Harris, Sydney 235
Harrison, Martha 191
Hartley, L. P. 74
Harwitz, Paul 227
Haskins, Ernest 30
Hastings, Selina 60
Hawkins, Paul 44
Hayakawa, S. I. 75

Hayes, Helen 28
Healey, Denis 204
Hedberg, Mitch 275
Heimel, Cynthia 238
Heine, Heinrich 193
Heller, Joseph 156
Hellman, Lillian 290
Helms, Jesse 211
Helpman, Robert 181
Hemingway, Ernest 90
Henry, Simon 180
Herbert, A.P. 12
Herold, Don 55, 257, 259
Heston, Charlton 138
Heyworth, Peter 174
Hicks, D. J. 161
Hightower, Cullen 211
Hill, Harry 96, 226, 234
Hill, Jimmy 274, 276
Hills, Dick 115
Hines, John 194
Hirschfeld, Al 13
Hirst, Damien 13, 19
Hitchcock, Alfred 137
Hoddle, Glenn 161
Hoffman, Abbie 206
Hoffnung, Gerard 296
Hoggart, Paul 285
Holden, William 86
Holiday, Billie 235
Homer Simpson 243
Hood, Thomas 61
Hope, Bob 30, 136, 139, 165, 271,
    272, 273, 276, 277, 287
Howard, Frankie 298
Howard, Michael 243
Howard, Philip 187
Howe, E. W. 33, 48, 67, 148
Howe, Gordie 264
Howse, Christopher 39
Hubbard, Elbert 19, 51

Hubbard, Kin 33, 67, 129, 148, 163,
    203, 246, 248
Humphrey, Hubert 213
Hunt, John 20
Huse, H. R. 56
Hyde-White, Wilfrid 292

Iannucci, Armando 93
Ibsen, Henrik 290, 303
Inge, William 221
Irons, Jeremy 140
Irwin, Wallace 91
Ivers, Molly 211
Izzard, Eddie 229

Jackson, Walthall 17
James, Brian 87
James, Dave 236
James, Henry 294
James, P. D. 188
Jarvis, Charles 60, 154
Jay, Anthony 210
Jaykus, Beth 110
Jeavons, Clyde 138
Jeni, Richard 227
Jessel, George 303
Joel, Billy 176
Johnson, Philip 18
Johnson, Samuel 41, 88, 187, 210
Johnson, Tony 268
Johnston, Paul 140
Jones, Clinton 35
Jones, Jack 201
Jones, Marie 177
Josipovich, Daniel 110
Josipovich, Dorothy 79
Judge, Elizabeth 264

Kahn, Alice 73, 118
Kaufman, George S. 287
Kaufman, Jean-Claude 113

Index

Kavanagh, Patrick 20, 196
Keating, Fred 247
Keating, Karen 163
Keats, John 83
Keegan, Kevin 155
Keillor, Garrison 43
Kelly, Charles 15
Kelly, Walt 233
Kennedy, Charles 205
Kenny, Jon 169
Kenny, Mary 261
Kerr, Walter 290
Kettle, Tom 56
Khalid, Haythum 237
Kidd, Jason 268
Kierkegaard, Soren 146
Kiley, Brian 51, 97, 114
King, Matt 227
King, Philip 288
Kipling, Rudyard 296
Kissinger, Henry 161
Klein, Allen 100
Klein, Steward 281
Klimek, Lester 105
Kline, Morris 229, 231
Klopstock, Friedrich 88
Knight, Eric 144
Knight, Greg 206
Kolinsky, Sue 193
Kraus, Karl 140, 185
Kurnitz, Harry 140

LaCava, Gregory 260
Lacey, David 145
Laing, R. D. 284
Lamarr, Hedy 180
Lamb, Charles 175
Lambert, Constant 188
Lambert, Jack 267
Lanchester, Elsa 144
Landesman, Cosmo 82

Landor, Walter Savage 248
Lange, Kelly 148
Langer, Agnes 118
Lansky, Bruce 50, 99, 100, 101, 229
Lapham, Lewis 243
Larkin, Philip 87, 187
Larson, Doug 253
Laurel, Stan 299
Lawrence, Gertrude 280
Lawrence, T. E. 299
Lawson, Nigella 48
Lawson, Sonia 15
Le Blanc, Jacques 294
Le Gallienne, Richard 86
Leacock, Stephen 164, 184, 229
Leary, Denis 43, 57, 61, 73, 118,
    168, 212, 246
Leavis, F. R. 86
Lebowitz, Fran 14, 62, 63, 88, 98,
    99, 102, 121, 185, 219, 231, 249
Lees-Milne, James 216
Lehrer, Tom 30, 193, 235
Leigh, Mark 132, 239
Leigh, Simon 57
Leonard, Hugh 28, 42, 135, 157,
    243, 286, 287
Leonard, Mike 275
Lepine, Mike 239
Lerner, Alan Jay 183
Leslie, Shane 45
Lester, Richard 144
Lette, Kathy 116, 155
Letterman, David 78, 184, 236
Levant, Oscar 20, 169, 171, 245
Levene, Malcolm 163
Levinson, Leonard 53, 76, 105, 122,
    234
Lewis, Jerry 281
Lewis, Joe E. 35, 40
Lewis, Sinclair 87
Lewis, Wyndham 247

 **Index**

Lewyt, Alex 238
Lieberman, Gerald F. 34
Lieberman, Max 15
Lilley, Peter 205
Lincoln, Abraham 15
Lipman, Maureen 181
Little, Mary 299
Lloyd-George, David 206
Loach, Ken 214
Lomas, Steve 277
Lombardi, Vince 265, 273
Long, J. L. 31
Lorenz, Konrad 233
Louis, Joe 268
Lovecraft, H. P. 302
Lucan, Arthur 97
Lujac, Larry 173
Lundquist, James 86
Lyle, Sandy 272
Lyon, Ben 30

Mabley, Moms 118
MacAleer, Kevin 219
Macaulay, Rose 252
Macauley, Robert B. 230
MacCampbell, Donald 85
MacDonald, Dwight 138
MacDonald, John D. 28
MacDougall, Donald 184
MacHale, Anne 127
MacHale, Des 64
MacHale, Dominic 160
Mackenzie, Compton 63
MacLean, Don 128
MacLiammoir, Michael 112
MacPherson, Archie 271
Madan, Geoffrey 42
Mailer, Norman 211
Maloney, Doris 171
Maltbie, Roger 270
Manning, Bernard 174, 192, 271

Marceau, Sophie 181
Maric, Silvio 196
Marshall, Arthur 90, 257
Marter, Barry 61
Martin, Dean 46, 145
Martin, Henry 34
Martin, Pete 233
Martin, Steve 256, 281
Marvin, Lee 122
Marx, Groucho 21, 25, 26, 61, 102,
    107, 116, 119, 139, 175, 193, 244,
    245, 251, 283, 302
Mason, Jackie 24, 31, 33, 35, 159
Mason, Roy 181
Masson, Tom 104
Matthau, Walter 112, 113, 137, 284
Maude, Chris 298
Maugham, Somerset 82, 288
Mavor, Michael 276
Maynard, John 72
Mays, Willie 265
McClue, Scott 123
McCormack, Mark 51
McCormack, Peter 249
McDonald, Gregory 150
McFarland, Thomas 51
McGee, Fibber 34
McGill, Donald 180
McGowan, Alistair 168
McGuigan, Barry 276
McIlroy, Sammy 162
McKeon, James 104, 220
McKeowan, John 289
McKeown, Jimeoin 180
McLaughty, James 252
McLeish, Henry 201, 297
McLuhan, Marshall 49
McNally, Frank 31
McQueen, Mike 85, 99, 117, 248
Meany, Goerge 72
Mellor, Anne 93

Mellor, David 72
Melly, George 170
Mencken, H. L. 73, 191, 210, 221, 222, 301
Mendosa, John 301
Menino, Thomas 185, 206
Meredith, George 253
Merlis, Bob 176
Merton, Paul 190, 202
Metalous, Grace 83
Metz, Milton 30
Michaels, Andrea 155
Midler, Bette 119, 259
Midwinter, Eric 174
Mikes, George 181
Mill, John Stuart 299
Miller, David 266
Miller, Dennis 117
Miller, Jon 229
Miller, Max 284
Milligan, Spike 148, 194, 295, 303
Mills, Bobby 294
Mills, Hugh 16
Milne, A. A. 242
Minoli, Angela 176
Minton, Bud 237
Mintzberg, Henry 29
Miss Piggy 67, 113
Mitchell, Julian 100
MItchell, Liz 269
Mitchum, Robert 137, 138, 139
Mizner, Addison 75, 79
Mizner, Wilson 45, 143, 259
Molière 163
Molnar, Ferenc 85
Montand, Yves 121
Montgomery, Bernard 16
Montgomery, James 222
Montgomery, Robert 135
Mooney, Sheila 83
Moore, George 83, 132, 292

Moore, Roger 96, 140
Moran, Aidan 236
Moran, Dylan 226
Morecambe, Eric 16, 271
Morgan, Piers 277
Morley, Robert 17, 35, 56, 57, 68, 69, 131, 190, 194, 195, 196, 197, 222, 260, 290, 303
Morley, Sheridan 83, 290
Morrison, Joe 190
Mortimer, John 50, 76, 154, 201, 294
Mortimer, Penelope 92
Moser, Leo 54
Mosley, Diana 203
Mountbatten, Philip 248
Muggeridge, Kitty 147
Muggeridge, Malcolm 86, 217, 258
Muir, Frank 60, 64, 155
Mull, Martin 45, 163
Mulligan, Hugh 63
Mumford, Ethel 244
Murdoch, Rupert 137
Murphy, Bill 237
Murphy, John 106, 257
Murphy, Robert 236
Murray, George 280
Murray, Jim 253
Murray, Mitch 17, 66, 91, 109, 127, 128, 129, 130, 222, 275
Murray, Patrick 84, 119, 123, 131, 143, 236, 266, 295, 297
Mussabini, Sam 275

Nansen, Fridtjof 192
Naryshnikov, Mikhail 281
Nash, Ogden 68, 103, 156, 158, 250
Nathan, George J. 135
Neilly, Jim 273
Nesbitt, Rab C. 42
Newby, David 193

Index

Nicely, Thomas 232
Nichols, Beverley 261
Nicholson, Jack 107
Nicklaus, Jack 269, 270
Nilsen, Aileen 228
Nimier, Roger 52
Niven, David 39, 143
Nkoloso, Edward 239
Norris, Alfred 130
Northcutt, Wendy 227, 295

O'Brien, Conan 134
O'Brien, Flann 52, 158, 186, 232
O'Connor, Sinead 216
O'Connor, Terry 266
O'Donovan, Peter 162
O'Gorman, Sian 151
O'Hanlon, Ardal 60, 96, 98
O'Mahony, Brendan 46
Onassis, Aristotle 29
O'Neill, Eugene 107
Orben, Robert 217
O'Rourke, Brian 41
O'Rourke, P. J. 69, 98, 104, 107,
    120, 182, 187, 189, 190, 204
Orton, Joe 121
Orwell, George 52, 85, 219
Osborne, John 135
Osgood, Peter 276
O'Shaughnessy, Don 210
O'Toole, Peter 149
Ovid 123

Parker, Dorothy 75, 86, 91, 107,
    112, 122, 145, 158, 222, 254, 258,
    290
Parker, Tom 176
Parks, Henry 206
Parr, Jack 134
Parsons, Nicholas 16
Parton, Dolly 114, 149

Patton, George 181, 299, 301
Paulos, John 226
Pearse, Lord 14
Pease, Allan 172
Peers, Joe 29
Pepys, Samuel 280
Percival, J. D. 233
Perelman, S. J. 25, 88, 134, 136, 158,
    246, 290
Peter, Laurence J. 75, 254
Peterson, Bill 277
Philips, Emo 27, 31, 65, 76, 106,
    126, 160, 188, 210, 259, 302, 304
Phillips, Bob 131, 152
Phillips, Leslie 300
Picasso, Pablo 12, 28
Pierrepoint, Albert 180
Pinker, Steven 170
Pirandello, Luigi 285
Plato 200
Player, Gary 104
Plomer, William 13
Plomp, John 101
Plummer, Christopher 150
Plunkett, James 219
Plunkitt, George 208
Podhoretz, John 82
Popper, Karl 55
'Posh Spice' 265
Potter, Maureen 242
Potter, Stephen 243
Poundstone, Paula 220
Powter, Susan 129
Pritchett, V. S. 260
Proust, Marcel 53
Pryor, Richard 108
Putin, Vladimir 201

Quarles, Francis 157
Quayle, Dan 93, 202, 209, 212, 237,
    296

Queensberry, Lord 250
Quelp, Henry 177
Quindlen, Anna 101
Quinn, Jimmy 267

Rabelais, François 164
Radner, Gilda 123
Raphael, Frederic 13, 290
Rather, Dan 77
Rattigan, Terence 112
Rattle, Simon 168
Rautianien, Pasi 45
Ray, Ted 269
Reagan, Ronald 208
Redmond, Michael 221
Reed, Oliver 125
Reed, Rex 249
Reichel, Carol 230
Reinhart, Ed 18
Renard, Jules 87
Renoir, Jean 149
Renoir, Pierre-Auguste 19
Richardson, Ralph 256
Rider, Steve 150
Ridge, William 244
Rifkind, Malcolm 205
Rivers, Joan 24, 66, 98, 103, 109,
    116, 118, 124, 128, 130, 135, 137,
    157, 196, 304
Roberts, George 294
Roberts, Graham 275
Robinson, Hercules 200
Robson, Bobby 169
Rodriguez, Chi Chi 270
Rogers, Will 20, 91, 148, 163, 204,
    208, 212, 295
Rooney, Mickey 32, 160
Roosevelt, Franklin 175
Roosevelt, Theodore 243
Root, Henry 145
Roque, Jacqueline 18

Rorem, Ned 16
Rosenberg, Joel 301
Ross, Harold 14
Ross, Jonathan 61
Rossini, Gioachino 177
Rossiter, Leonard 75
Rosten, Norman 294
Roth, David 170
Rousseau, Jean-Jacques 176
Rowland, Helen 120, 122, 131, 261
Roy, Dixy Lee 238
Rubin, Jerry 219
Rudner, Rita 78, 113, 115, 116,
    149, 211, 222, 239
Rushton, Willie 64
Russell, Bertrand 44, 217, 228

Saki 121, 159, 216, 251, 284
Salinger, J. D. 220, 230
Saltus, Edgar 132
Sandburg, Carl 141
Sanders, George 202
Sansom, Ruth 104
Santayana, George 53
Sayle, Alexei 213
Schaffer, Bob 30
Schoenberg, Arnold 20
Schroeder, Patricia 207
Schwarzenegger, Arnold 29
Secombe, Harry 304
Sedaris, David 188
Seinfeld, Jerry 16, 31, 38, 76, 89,
    107, 120, 124, 127, 139, 145, 146,
    172, 233, 254, 255, 256, 258, 272,
    299, 300
Selznick, David 149
Shackleton, Len 265
Shackleton, Lord 209
Shankly, Bill 264, 270, 274
Sharp, Dolph 30, 250
Shaw, George Bernard 24, 51, 67,

168, 172, 173, 186, 219, 250, 252, 273, 284, 285
Shenstone, William 277
Shepard, Sam 142, 143
Sheridan, Richard Brinsley 26, 57
Shore, Dinah 169
Shorten, Caroline 202
Shulman, Milton 221
Sickert, Walter 245
Signoret, Simone 135
Simon, John 139, 149, 150
Simon, Neil 63
Simon, Paul 177
Simpson, Bart 74
Simpson, Homer 243
Simpson, James 302
Simpson, Wallis 28
Singer, Isaac 303
Skinner, Cornelia Otis 156
Skinner, Dennis 204
Skinner, Frank 146
Sladek, John 230
Sledge, Tommy 295
Sloan, John 16
Sloane, Paul 33
Smirnoff, Yakov 44
Smith, Adam 56
Smith, F. H. 209
Smith, Logan Pearsall 109, 261
Smith, Patti 218
Smith, Sydney 51, 57, 89, 154, 185
Smith, Wallace 144
Snead, Sam 147
Soaper, Joseph 123
Sokolov, Raymond 187
Spark, Muriel 123, 216
Sparrow, John 90
Speicher, Eugene 14
Spendlove, Scott 99
St Augustine 119
Stanshall, Vivian 41

Stead, Christina 103
Steel, Mark 55
Steffens, Lincoln 141
Stein, Leo 21
Stephen, Jaci 160
Stevenson, Melford 192
Stone, Sharon 126
Stoppard, Tom 192, 282
Strachan, Gordon 145
Strachey, John 219
Strachey, Lytton 82
Strang, Ivan 54
Streisand, Barbra 286
Swenson, John 172

Talleyrand, Charles de 122
Tan, Alex 164
Taylor, A. J. P. 136
Taylor, Elizabeth 139, 255
Tennyson, Alfred 90
Thatcher, Carol 82
Thatcher, Margaret 203, 214
Theroux, Paul 203
Thiers, Louis 246
Thirbell, Angela 93
Thomas, Dylan 12
Thompson, Dan 77, 256
Thomson, David 137
Thoreau, Henry David 150
Thurber, James 96, 132, 144, 284
Tibballs, Geoff 12, 155, 244
Tierney, Joe 165
Titian 12
Tomlin, Lily 164, 196, 274
Took, Barry 281
Toscanini, Arturo 171
Toscano, Harry 264
Townsend, Robert 24
Trevino, Lee 264, 271
Trillin, Calvin 68
Trinder, Tommy 185

Trollope, Joanna 89
Trotter, Wilfred 158
Trueman, Fred 91
Trumbo, Dalton 195
Trump, Ivana 24
Tucholsky, Kurt 187
Turnbull, Heather 182
Twain, Mark 14, 15, 33, 50, 85, 104, 106, 113, 157, 176, 182, 183, 212, 217, 218, 242, 250
Twomey, Brian 234
Tynan, Kenneth 287
Tyson, Mike 264

Underhill, Frank 200
Unwin, Stanley 27
Updike, John 29, 139
Ustinov, Peter 296, 298

Van Horne, Harriet 151
Varano, Frank 44, 65
Vaughan, Bill 55, 211, 248
Verdi, Giuseppe 171
Victor, Paula 286
Victoria, Queen 203, 287
Vidal, Gore 92, 187, 244
Vidor, King 137
Vine, David 276
Viorst, Judith 62
Voltaire 164, 252
Von Neumann, John 232

Waas, Sam 142
Wagner, Richard 171
Walden, George 41
Walker, Murray 266, 267, 268
Wall, Max 281
Waller, Edmund 92
Wallis, Richard 186
Walpole, Horace 213
Walton, Sam 29

Warfield, Marsha 245
Warner, Jack 150
Waterhouse, Keith 184, 207
Waugh, Auberon 51, 88, 103, 120, 186, 208, 210
Waugh, Evelyn 19, 38, 39, 48, 73, 82, 84, 97, 180, 196, 216, 246, 252, 294
Wax, Ruby 30
Wayne, John 42, 136
Weil, André 232
Wells, Bob 213
Werb, Mike 116
West, Mae 28, 112, 115, 122, 247, 281, 292
West, Rebecca 90, 251
Whistler, James McNeill 14, 15, 20
White, Paula 174
White, Ronald 151
Whitehorn, Katherine 249
Whittel, Giles 189
Wiggan, A.E. 53
Wilde, Oscar 17, 18, 48, 50, 90, 129, 158, 189, 192, 195, 245, 249, 254, 255, 256, 257, 258, 260, 286, 288
Wilder, Billy 147, 285, 295
Wilensky, Robert 233
Will, George 209
Willans, Geoffrey 93
Williams, Esther 148
Williams, Jimmy 113
Williams, Kenneth 288
Williams, Pat 277
Williams, Robin 25, 120, 127, 221, 297
Willis, Bruce 126
Wilson, A. N. 197
Wilson, Bryan 50
Wilson, N. 79
Wilson, Woodrow 48
Winner, Michael 60, 61

Index

Winslet, Kate 142
Winstead, Liz 117
Winters, Shelley 160
Wise, Denis 269
Wise, Ernie 174
Wodehouse, P. G. 288
Wogan, Terry 136
Womersley, David 50
Wood, Gordon 270
Wood, Victoria 123
Woods, Tiger 264
Woollcott, Alexander 161, 216
Woolley, Hannah 52
Wordsworth, Christopher 134
Wray, Fay 150
Wright, Frank Lloyd 75, 188
Wright, Ian 43, 274
Wright, Steven 18, 19, 26, 52, 72,
    74, 75, 100, 101, 156, 165, 170,
    230, 234, 235, 237, 247, 296, 297,
    298, 302, 303
Wuhl, Robert 170

Yeltsin, Boris 183
Young, Chic 126
Youngman, Henny 34, 35, 45, 62,
    64, 78, 108, 125, 128, 130, 154,
    175, 254, 302
Yucel, Can 208

Zappa, Frank 18, 19
Zellerbach, Merla 60
Ziegler, Larry 96
Ziglar, Zig 172
Zito, Nick 264